True Religion

Blackwell Manifestos

In this new series major critics make timely interventions to address important concepts and subjects, including topics as diverse as, for example: Culture, Race, Religion, History, Society, Geography, Literature, Literary Theory, Shakespeare, Cinema, and Modernism. Written accessibly and with verve and spirit, these books follow no uniform prescription but set out to engage and challenge the broadest range of readers, from undergraduates to postgraduates, university teachers and general readers – all those, in short, interested in ongoing debates and controversies in the humanities and social sciences.

True Religion

Graham Ward

Blackwell
Publishing

350 Main Street, Malden, MA 02148-5018, USA
108 Cowley Road, Oxford OX4 1JF, UK
550 Swanston Street, Carlton South, Victoria 3053, Australia
Kurfürstendamm 57, 10707 Berlin, Germany

First published 2003 by Blackwell Publishers Ltd, a Blackwell Publishing company

Library of Congress Cataloging-in-Publication Data
Ward, Graham.
    True religion / Graham Ward.
       p. cm. – (Blackwell manifestos)
  Includes bibliographical references and index.
     ISBN 0-631-22173-5 (alk. paper) – ISBN 0-631-22174-3 (pbk.: alk. paper)
     1. Religion. I. Title. II. Series.
  BL48. W189 2003
  200–dc21

                                                                2002004861

A catalogue record for this title is available from the British Library.

Set in 11.5/13.5pt Bembo
by Graphicraft Limited, Hong Kong
Printed and bound in the United Kingdom
by MPG Books Ltd, Bodmin, Cornwall

For further information on
Blackwell Publishing, visit our website:
http://www.blackwellpublishing.com

Contents

Acknowledgements

I doubt I would have written this book at all had I not moved to the University of Manchester and worked alongside colleagues in a department of Religions and Theology and become involved with the Centre for Religion, Culture and Gender. Besides these colleagues, as any teacher knows, much is owed to one's students. A good student can be better than any number of scholarly books, for the questions they bring and the elucidations they demand. Thinking is pushed forward. I have been fortunate in having had a number of such students. To name individuals would be insidious, but I hope if they read this book they may themselves recognize their contributions. I have also been fortunate in having in Andrew McNeillie an editor who encouraged me to believe what this book might turn into. I want to thank each of them for the sense I had throughout this book of a co-operative venture.

Introduction: A Manifesto

Religion is, once more, haunting the imagination of the West. The various attempts to exorcise its presence – from Feuerbach's anthropology to Freudian psychology, from the atheism of the logical atomists to the quarantining policies of liberalism – have failed, for the secularism upon which they were each founded is imploding. A new remythologizing of the real – media-driven, market-led – is emerging. But what does the appearance of this spectre at the end of the twentieth and the beginning of the twenty-first centuries portend? ' "Religious sentiment" is itself a social product', the seventh of Marx's theses on Feuerbach states. And while this was yet another attempt to expunge the transcendent, it points to where critical analysis must begin: with the social production of the religious. What then is being produced in and through contemporary religion and why? Furthermore, having understood something of the cultural logic of this present production, what are its implications for the future?

The answer to these questions can only issue from an historical analysis of the cultural embeddedness of 'religion'. We stand today in a place created from the manifold labours of human beings and social institutions. We have to examine material practices, and how those practices wrought changes; how they were produced and productive. For we stand in the trajectory of the history of the social production of religion. And not only religion, but also discursive practices closely related to religion (like faith, belief and theology) and practices antithetical – yet for that reason still closely related to – the changing understanding of religion (like secularism and modernity). We need a genealogy in which the role played by religion – from the voyages of discovery to the Holy Land Experience theme park in Florida and the aggressive convictions of fundamentalists – can be assessed.

The genealogy I offer charts the changes in the understanding of 'true religion' from Shakespeare to Salman Rushdie, pointing out how closely linked those changes are to the waxing and waning of modernity and the increasing incursions on the social and the cultural of global capitalism. In turn such changes are related to the rise, development and, finally, implosion of the secularist worldview. Marx, in those same theses on Feuerbach, observed the virtual reality of secularism: 'For the fact that the secular foundation detaches itself from itself and establishes itself in the clouds as an independent realm is really to be explained only by the self-cleavage and self-contradictoriness of this secular basis.' He called for the removal of the contradictory basis through a revolution in practice. The genealogy I offer is an attempt at such a practice. Rather than stabilizing the secular foundation (as Marx desired), this genealogy wishes to demonstrate how secularism's virtual reality is recognizing itself as such. And the various pursuits for 'true religion' today are living, practical consequences of such a recognition.

That genealogy allows me to make the following claims:

- What we are witnessing in Western culture today is the liquidation of 'religion' through its commodification.
- This liquidation is the outworking of a cultural logic in which 'religion' was inseparable from an imperialistic drive fundamental to Christian missiology and the development of world-trade systems.
- 'Religion' is a defining characteristic of postmodernity, testifying to the implosion of both secularism and liberalism and the re-enchantment of the world.
- The implosion of both secularism and liberalism is also the outworking of logics at the core of their enterprises.
- Contemporary Western postsecularism and postliberalism fetishizes all values and objects such that 'religion' has become *the*

commodified 'special effect'. Religion baptises this fetishizing with the allure of a cheap transcendence.

- With the translation of values into market-developed lifestyles we are close to the dissolving of the social into the cultural, sociality into neo-tribalism.
- One of the strong reactions to this tendency has been a return to theological traditions and tradition-based forms of reasoning.
- It is difficult to see what resources there are outside of theological traditions, opposed to phantasms of commercial 'religion', for preventing the collapse of society into culture, the social into the neo-tribal.
- The theological voice will have a much higher profile in public debates and the production of public truth.
- The turn to theology offers the only possible future for faith traditions, but this will in turn increasingly generate culture wars, as the politics of politeness are erased by the radical politics of difference.
- At the moment, the major cultural wars are between faith communities and the remnants of the secular, liberal worldview. This will change. In their new self-assertiveness these faith communities might then turn upon each other.
- The possibilities for resolving these culture wars lie with each theological tradition negotiating the pressure to fetishize their faith.

The story that follows offers a demonstration of these claims.

1

Religion Before and After Secularism

Implosion is not the 'end' of secularism, as postmodernity is not the 'end' of modernity and postliberalism is not the end of liberalism. There are no radical breaks or ruptures culturally, only negotiations that modify in rehearsing what has been received. Just as the Georgian and Victorian squares and the 1960s examples of office-block modernism remain in the transforming urban landscape, so secularism has its institutions – its systems of education, its practices of law, its government statutes, its research laboratories. These will maintain the myths of objective, impartial knowledge and judgements by quarantining theistic belief-practices for some time to come. They will continue to promote human autonomy and the democratic ideal in terms of the rights of 'man'. What the implosion signals is that secularism is coming to an end; that modernity is being undermined from within by a certain dawning realization of its unstable foundations; and that liberalism's universalism, egalitarianism and belief in progress are in terminal decline.

These observations, let me quickly add, are not to be taken as outright condemnations of secularism or modernity or liberalism. Much violence, atrocity, oppression and sheer waste of human resources have been the product of so much religious bigotry, so many different kinds of 'wars of religion'. Even today it might be remarked that in certain countries in the world a good dose of secularism would break the repressive holds certain state-ratified religions have over people's lives. Nor can we say that nothing good came from modernity, or that nothing good still comes from its traditions. The fruits of modernity in terms of the pursuit of humanitarian principles, the advances in medicine and science, and the promotion of educational and political ideals are evident: in public libraries, schools, universities, hospitals, law courts, etc. The observation I am making in this manifesto is that there is a deepening crisis of secularism, modernity and liberal values, such that our culture – being elsewhere – finds some of the assumptions and presuppositions of secularism, modernity and liberalism no longer credible. I am talking about credibility here, not what is true and what is false. I have no view from above; religions have no unmediated, unambivalent view from above either. We – and by that I mean not only we in North America and Western Europe, but we who in these geographic locations have had and continue to have profound influence over the rest of the world – are in the midst of a cultural sea-change.

One of the most striking characteristics of that sea-change is the return of religion to the public arena and the consumer market. However, we are moving too quickly here, and much of this will have to be revisited in the final chapter, where I try to present a description of where we are and what this might imply about where we are going.

Cultural Hermeneutics

For now, we have some fairly weighty words on the textual table: 'religion', 'secularism', 'modernity', 'postmodernity' and 'liberalism'. I am shortly going to add another: 'theology'. I am not going to define any of these terms. There are enough studies that offer tours of how *religio* has its roots in the classical Roman *relegere*, 'to reread', or *legere*, 'to gather', and so is synonymous with *traditio*. The third-century Christian writer Lactantius relates 'religion' to *religare*, 'to bind up' or 'to bind together', and so religion becomes inseparable from liturgy, community and the practice of faith. *Religio* is 'worship of the true' – with the explicit reminder that only Christianity is therefore a religion, the 'true religion'. In his treatise *de vere religione* Augustine concurred.

2

Theology has a more ancient pedigree. The use of *theologia* to describe stories about or thought concerning the gods is found in Plato and Aristotle. It is not found in the New Testament and *theologia*, like *religio*, underwent a Christian appropriation, having been at first avoided by the early church writers because of its associations with 'paganism'. When appropriated by figures such as Athenagorus and Clement of Alexandria, 'theology' did not refer to knowledge of God's nature, but speaking about the God who is believed in. Theology was synonymous with doxology.

Furthermore, *saeculum* came to mean 'age', 'this age', 'the present world' and, finally, 'an account of the world without reference to God'. *Modus* means 'now' and the concerns with the present rather than the traditions of the past; and so 'modernity' as a cultural epoch characterized by rethinking the present and the future independently of the past is antagonistic to religion as *relegere* and *traditio*. *Postmodus* can mean either 'after the modern', 'anterior to the modern' or both, as Jean-François Lyotard has taught us.

I am not going to proceed by taking off-the-shelf definitions founded upon etymological possibilities. The importance of drawing attention to the semantic histories of these key terms is to show how words slip and slide in their different uses. What will become evident is how these words are exchanged and circulate in specific cultural and historical contexts, each impacting upon the other. They are defined and redefined as they are iterated in this novel, in that play, in this tract, in that journal entry, across time. Each iteration is an interpretation and a new cultural negotiation. It is by means of these interpretations that cultures change internally and modify each other. Hence what this book seeks to uncover is something of the cultural hermeneutics in which religion, theology and the secular participate. So, in order to understand both what 'true religion' produces and how it is itself part of a cultural production, we need to observe where 'religion' makes its appearance within particular cultural matrices and begin to analyse the nature and significance of those appearances within those specific contexts. We can then allow the nature of what is 'religion' to emerge from the cultural appearance it has made and the nexus of associations in which it stands. In this way we investigate its formations and transformations as a discourse – that is, the way the word is articulated

3

within specific gestures, actions, speaking and writings, and the institutions that govern, evaluate and enforce those articulations.

This investigation is not in terms of cause and effect. We are not tracing the influence of 'religion' on literature, say, or the influence of state power on the constitution of 'religion'. We are examining the networks of exchange of signs and the cultural fluidity involved in those networks, such that attempts to determine the direction of influence, the mechanics of cause and effect, are understood as too reductive, too restrictive. 'True religion' is disseminated across social and historical processes; the poetics and politics of cultural determination, production and transformation. What is achieved by analysing this dissemination between, say, the fourteenth and the twenty-first centuries, is a certain genealogy of 'religion'. Cultural hermeneutics enables a story to be constructed, a narrative in which we can appreciate the way the word 'religion' and the pursuit of the 'true religion' are produced, challenged and transformed. We can present these exchanges and negotiations only through examining particular events or cultural loci, making evident the worldview or cultural imaginary that constitutes and is constituted by these events. Frequently these events or loci will be literary texts or other cultural forms such as buildings and films, since in these 'events' or loci are often found complex expressions of the way the world is experienced and understood. We can 'ask how collective beliefs and experiences were shaped, moved from one medium to another, concentrated in manageable aesthetic forms, offered for consumption'[1] and gained popular approval.

The transformation of 'religion' will have implications for other terms: the secular, modernity, postmodernity and theology. For the early developments of secularism in England have been traced to the use made of Protestant thinking in Henry VIII's famous dissolution of the monasteries in the sixteenth century. The early development of 'modernism' has been discerned in the penchant among scholastics of the high Middle Ages for the free exercise of the speculative intellect – free, that is, from appeals to authorities such as the scriptures and the reflections of the church Fathers and ecumenical councils (mediated, it is true, by the cultural politics of the church). From these scholastic freedoms the shift from Oxford University's motto *dominus illuminatio meo* to Enlightenment rationalism was triggered and likewise the inauguration of the modern. No doubt both these genealogies

4

require critical attention, but the change I wish to illustrate in this chapter is that which occurs between pre- and postmodern religion, at a time when secularism's star was in the ascendant.

Romeo and Juliet I

We will begin at a performance of Shakespeare's *Romeo and Juliet*, or a particular reading of it, which took place at the Globe Theatre probably in the season 1594–5. My reading of the play is influenced in part by a certain perspective being investigated by contemporary Shakespearian scholars: Shakespeare's relations with Roman Catholicism.[2] Shakespeare's father, after all, is known now to have been a recusant; that is, a Catholic who refused to go to the newly formed and constituted Protestant Church of England brought about by the Elizabethan Settlement. Shakespeare himself may be the same 'William Shakeshafte' who served in one of the great Catholic houses in Lancashire during the 1580s. The focus of my critical attention will therefore be upon (1) the role of Friar Laurence, (2) the role the sacraments play with respect to the politics of personal love and civic strife within the play, and (3) religious rhetoric as it is used by various characters. I am attempting to reconstruct what was understood by religion at a certain time, in a certain context.

The opening of the play establishes an atmosphere of sexual pleasure and violent struggle, dominant throughout. Swords become pricks and pricks become swords in a fluid metamorphosis that requires no Freudian analysis. The entrance of the brooding Romeo only intensifies the youthful, turbulent erotics, by demonstrating through the excessiveness of his love for Rosaline the profound internalization of these feuding dynamics, this 'brawling love'. He participates in the fray, despite not being present at the recent squabble. And religious references constantly appear, in ways that do not draw attention to themselves at this point, but weave in and out of the feverish antitheses of desire and aggression, libidinal pleasures and murderous impulsiveness. The 'fiery Tybalt' hates the Montagues as much as he hates hell; the Capulet characters who provoke the opening fight bear ironized biblical names: Sampson the Old Testament Judge; Abram the Jewish lawgiver; and Balthasar, a name given by legend to one of the three wise men who brought gifts to lay at the feet of the infant Christ. Prince Escalus equates, in true Elizabethan fashion, rebellion with profanity; Benvolio acts as Romeo's confessor, hearing his 'true shrift'; Rosaline repudiates Romeo's advances because she has taken a vow of chastity, wishing either to remain in or enter a convent; and Benvolio wishes to teach Romeo another 'doctrine'. But it is within the poetry of Romeo's early ruminations that religion is not only first named, but appears as a defining characteristic of the cultural context:

> Why then, O brawling love, O loving hate
> O anything of nothing first create!
> O heavy lightness, serious vanity,
> Misshapen chaos of well-seeming forms! (I.1, 174–7)

Here Romeo relates the play's violent erotics to the creation of the world out of the brooding chaos of nothingness described in the opening lines of Genesis. The violences, though, are clouding the creative processes, so that he (and we) are unsure of the procedure – does chaos move towards well-seeming forms (in which case why the 'seeming'?), does anything come from nothing (in which case why the 'vanity'?), or is it all the other way around and are the divine creative processes being reversed? In making this metaphoric connection Romeo expands the local libidinal warfare shattering the peace of Verona to embrace the cosmic creativity of divine love – the love that shapes all times and places. Romeo intuitively acknowledges a providence, a divine economy at work in creation and maintaining the world. His personal perplexity, expressive of a wider internecine struggle, has not simply a religious dimension, but is itself essentially religious. And so he concludes his deliberations with Benvolio:

> When the devout religion of mine eye
> Maintains such falsehood, then turn tears to fire,
> And these who, often drown'd, could never die,
> Transparent heretics, be burnt for liars. (I.2, 90–3)

Of course, the references to religion and religious acts here are metaphorical. But Shakespeare's metaphors have both a habit of translating themselves into social and historical events on stage and mirroring social and historical events off stage. The trials and persecution of both Catholics and Protestants as heretics had been very much part of the English Christian religion since the death of Henry VIII. Such trials and persecutions were not simply memories. Throughout Elizabeth's reign there were intense purges of Catholics as treasonous plots were uncovered or threats of invasion or usurpation loomed. Some of Shakespeare's friends, family and patrons were implicated in harbouring Catholic priests (a capital offence) and plotting against the queen. The years following the execution of Mary Queen of Scots (1587), the years in which Shakespeare wrote *Romeo and Juliet* and was closely associated with the Earl of Southampton (son of an ardent Catholic who had died imprisoned in the Tower for his faith), were years of aggressive persecution. In March and September of 1592 the name of Shakespeare's own father, John, appeared twice among lists of recusants. Romeo's complex conceit, in which devotion is both true and heretic, rehearses not only the wider theatrical action, but an action which frames and makes that theatrical action possible. 'True religion' was embedded in a culture of violent hatreds; the Christian gospel of love was preached with the threats not of hell's fires only, but earthly fires also and instruments of torture. Erasmus's 'Prayer for the Peace of the Churche' (reprinted in Henry VIII's 1545 *Primer*) defines an ethos in which there is 'no charite, no fidelite, no bondes of love, no reverence, neither lawes nor yet of rulers, no agreement of opinions, but as it were in a misordered quire, every man singeth, a contrary note'. The warring between the Montagues and Capulets, a warring without origin or even a focus – a nameless, causeless warring – reflects Erasmus's sentiment and is reflected in Romeo's early ruminations.

The word 'religion' was itself being redefined in and through the turbulence engendered by the politics of Puritan and Catholic demands for reformation and counter-reformation and the rise of the nascent state. The continual search to define the true faith – expressed in documents such as the 1542 'Act for the Advancement of True Religion' – was a search to define a new cultural sensibility. We will say more about this in the next chapter. Suffice it here to point out that it has been argued that the so-called 'Wars of Religion' that occupied the best resources of Western Europe for almost two centuries involved the production of the modern concept of 'religion'. This said, the restless antagonisms over the true faith that led eventually to the bloody Thirty Years War (see chapter 2) were manifest much earlier, and that part of what we are witnessing in the mid-1590s' composition of *Romeo and Juliet* is a participation in the circulation of social energies at that time in which 'religion' figured prominently. As such, the word 'religion' takes on the colouring and contents of the practices, events and institutions which embody, police and produce the 'religious' understanding of persons, communities, circumstances, pasts, presents and futures. With *Romeo and Juliet* we are examining a critical moment of theological and political confusion and the search for a way beyond it.

It is the house of Capulet that establishes the dominant Catholic worldview that had been England's past and was now passing away. Touches of nostalgia mark the early scenes in the Capulet household. Juliet's father proposes to hold 'an old accustomed feast', akin to the feast held one Pentecost that he recalls in conversation with his cousin. Dating seems very important here. It has been noted how in the sources for the play (Brooke's *The Tragicall Historye of Romeus and Juliet* (1562) and Painter's *novella* on Romeo and Juliet in the second volume of his *Palace of Pleasure* (1580)) the feast takes place just before Christmas. But Shakespeare transposes the feast (which Tybalt twice calls a 'solemnity', a word quite specifically used with respect to holy days) and the events of the play to mid-July, as Juliet approaches her fourteenth birthday on 1 August. In whose honour the Capulet feast is celebrated is left unclear. July is the month of six important feasts – of St Thomas à Becket (7th), of St Swithun (15th), of St Margaret (21st), of St Mary Magdalene (22nd), of St James the Apostle (25th) and St Anne (26th). There is a specific dating of the feast in the conversation between the nurse and Lady Capulet: 'a fortnight and odd days' from Lammas, which suggests the old accustomed feast is on St Swithun's Day. St Swithun's Day marked the onset of the summer storms and it may well have been presented on stage by some symbolic prop. Summer storms could have devastating consequences on harvests and it was said that if it rained on St Swithun's Day it would rain for forty days thereafter. Harvests might have to be gathered early, before their prime.

Perhaps the reason for not mentioning the saint's day by name has something to do with the fact that in 1532 Cromwell (vice-regent in spirituals) and Henry VIII had passed the Act for the Abrogation of Certain Holy Days. This put an end to liturgical time by demanding that people work through from 1 July to 29 September and disregard certain saints' feast days, partly on the grounds of fighting sloth and idleness and partly on the grounds of the sins of excess and riot 'being entysed by the laity'. All the feasts in July were abrogated except for that of St James the Apostle, including the festival of Lammas. This was another important date in the calendar. It was an old pagan festival that Christianity had baptised (and no doubt related in Shakespeare to the folklore narratives of Queen Mab). Lammas marked the end of summer and the beginning of autumn. It was a harvest festival, for the word comes from 'loaf-mass'. On this day loaves of bread were baked from the first grain of the harvest and laid on the church altars as sacrificial offerings. It was a day representative of 'first fruits'. We will return to the association of Juliet with sacrifice and the eucharist later, only observing here that Romeo, like Juliet, was a first and only born. Lammas was also the favoured day for the feast of St Catherine. The action of the play then takes place within the liturgical calendar, itself part of the seasonal cycle.

The Nurse's colloquialisms offer an important insight into the speech of the Catholic commoner, with her 'God rest all Christian souls', 'by th' rood', 'by my holidame' and 'God mark thee to his grace'. But they also help to blur the distinction between the sacred spaces of court and church. In fact, a liturgical fluidity between court, theatre and church is evident that finds its clearest expression in the first encounter between Romeo and Juliet at the 'solemnity':

Romeo: If I profane with my unworthiest hand
This holy shrine, the gentle sin is this:
My lips, two blushing pilgrims, ready stand
To smooth that rough touch with a tender kiss.
Juliet: Good pilgrim, you do wrong your hand too much,
Which mannerly devotion shows in this;
And palm to palm is holy palmers' kiss.
Romeo: Have not saints lips, and holy palmers too?

9

Juliet: Ay, pilgrim, lips that they must use in prayer.
Romeo: O then, dear saint, let lips do what hands do:
         They pray: grant thou, lest faith turn to despair.
Juliet: Saints do not move, though grant for prayer's sake.
Romeo: Then move not, while my prayer's effect I take.
         Thus from my lips, by thine, my sin is purg'd.
Juliet: Then have my lips the sin that they have took.
Romeo: Sin from my lips? O trespass sweetly urg'd.
         Give me my sin again.
Juliet: You kiss by th' book. (I.5, 92–109)

Romeo's erstwhile mention of 'religion' has now become his 'faith'. As Aquinas expressed it in article 3 of *quaestio* 81 of his *Summa Theologiae*, 'true religion professes faith in one God'. Drawing on the connection made in the New Testament epistle of St James, religion is understood as worship and service. It is a moral action devoted to pious ends, Aquinas argues:

> Religion has two kinds of acts. Some are its proper and immediate acts, which it elicits, and by which man is directed to God alone, for instance, sacrifice, adoration and the like. But it has other acts, which it produces through the medium of the virtues which it commands, directing them to the honour of God, because the virtue which is concerned with the end, commands the virtues which are concerned with the means.

Religion is the virtuous practice of the faith. In fact 'faith', rather than 'religion', was the dominant appellation throughout premodernity. Wilfred Cantwell Smith observes: 'no one, so far as I have been able to ascertain, ever wrote a book specifically on "religion" [in the Middles Ages]'.[3] It was Protestantism, and Calvin in particular, whose most disseminated work was entitled *Christianae Religionis Institutio*, which popularized the term *religio*, Smith argues. Interestingly, and significantly, Calvin's earlier work of 1537 was entitled *Instruction et Confession de Foy* – equating *religio* with *foi* – religion with faith. At this point, then, the term retained its older associations: a 'religious' was one devoted to the practice of piety, one who was often in holy orders. 'Although the name "religious" may be given to all in general who worship God, yet in a special way religious are those who consecrate their whole life to the Divine worship, by withdrawing from human affairs', Aquinas stated. The term *religio* was also beginning to be employed politically to distinguish Protestantism from Roman Catholicism, as is evident in Zwingli's 1525 *Commentarius de vera et falsa religion*. By 1547, Cranmer's *Homily of Good Works* can speak of 'ungodly and counterfeit religions', by which he means 'papistical superstitions and abuses'.[4] 'True religion' was the right practice of the faith – a practice not founded upon superstitions or folktales – and it was not a practice viewed primarily as a clerical or monastic one.

The stirrings of love in Romeo once more invoke religious metaphor; but here not *simply* metaphor. What Juliet calls forth is also religious gesture and practice. This liturgical cameo serves not only to lift and isolate the couple above the crowded festivities; it serves also to solemnize their exchange, producing a sacred space that transfigures the ordinary. The appeal to the Catholic veneration of saints, the intercession of saints, sacramental confession and the significance of pilgrimage ring nostalgically. There had been wave upon wave of iconoclastic wrath since Henry VIII's dissolution of the monasteries and the raiding of reliquaries. The three great pilgrimage sites of England (Walsingham, Ipswich and Canterbury) had been plundered and empty niches in many a parish church testified to the disappearance of the saints. Veneration of holy things was explicitly forbidden by the 22nd of the 39 Articles agreed upon by the archbishops and bishops in 1563 and subscription to which was required of all clergy in the Church of England: 'The Romish doctrine concerning purgatory, pardons, worshipping and adoration as well of images as of relics, and also the invocation of saints, is a fond thing, vainly invented, and grounded upon no warrant of scripture, but rather repugnant to the word of God.' And yet here Romeo constructs Juliet as a 'holy shrine', while courtly etiquette ('You kiss by th' book') and theatrical production fuse with a liturgical act of devotion. Later, in the balcony scene, in which Juliet is again invoked as 'dear saint', the liturgical act of naming, baptism, is rehearsed and they come close to a solemn exchange of vows. If at the end of the balcony scene the liturgy of their encounter does not conclude with their being one flesh, they are one soul – as Romeo recognizes.

11

It is this easy transit between different symbolic worlds which is significant. The transits are marked (as in this exchange between Romeo and Juliet or the scene between the Nurse and Lady Capulet) by a certain levity or playfulness. We find this fluidity throughout the play, where sexual innuendo and true affection, the worlds of nature and of church, intermingle. The Elizabethan social world was one such that a hat worn by Cardinal Wolsey could end up as a prop in a theatrical cupboard. The fluidity stands in dramatic contrast to the jarring clashes of feuding passions – it is the contrast that produces and drives the dramatic action itself. However (and this is where *Romeo and Juliet* fits uneasily into the tragic worldview), the play moves inexorably towards a resolution. Like *A Midsummer Night's Dream*, the play moves towards the overcoming of the conflictual and not just the restoration but the full realization of the interrelation of different worlds. Fundamentally, the vision behind this interconnectedness is a sacramental one – a Catholic cosmology in which the secular is not a distinct realm of socio-economic and political operations, but a realm suffused with divine activities. Romeo's allusion to the present confusion in the relation between creation and chaos is corrected by Juliet's recognition that what her encounter with Romeo has delivered is a certain impregnation. In terms which seem to echo both a Marian role and the sentiments of Christ, she speaks of a 'Prodigious birth of love it is to me / That I must love a loathed enemy'. Both of them are caught up in a divine comedy in which together they will temper extremities. And hence realms terrestrial and celestial, spheres and stars and seas and angels, frame the poetry of their love.

The sacramental worldview is given full expression on the entry of Friar Laurence:

> O, mickle is the powerful grace that lies
> In plants, herbs, stones, and their true qualities.
> For naught so vile that on the earth doth live
> But to the earth some special good doth give.

Shakespeare's sympathetic treatment of the Friar is in contrast to the Protestant vilification of friars in Brooke's preface to the readers of his tale: 'superstitious friars (the naturally fitte instruments of unchastity)' are listed along with 'dronken gossypes'. But, significantly, the tone of the preface differs markedly from Brooke's much more approving portrait of the Friar in the narration. Brooke recognizes, like Shakespeare, that the Friar is both the dramatic catalyst for the ensuing events and the guarantor of peace and friendship between Montague and Capulet. The Friar announces the bond of religious and civic unity:

> The bounty of the fryer and wisdom hath so wonnne
> The townes folks herts, that welnigh all to fryer Lawrence
> ronne
> To shrive them selfe the olde, the yong, the great and small.
> Of all he is beloved well, and honord much of all.
> And for he did the rest in wisdome farre exceede,
> The Prince by him (his counsell cravde) was holpe at time
> of neede.
> Betwixt the Capilets and him great frendship grew:
> A secret and assured frend unto the Montegue.

The sacramental worldview the Friar embodies and practises (as priestly confessor, physician of soul and body, and celebrant of baptismal, nuptial and burial rites) is the foundation for his roles as mediator and peace-maker. He not only interrelates the natural, commoner, courtly and ecclesial worlds; his movements across them makes possible the fluid transits between these worlds that we have noted. His use of invocations ('Benedictite', 'God pardon sin', 'Holy Saint Francis!' and 'Jesu Maria!') betrays the source of the Nurse's own speaking. Both are intercessory figures, figures relating and working for the sublation of factions. But the Friar is the focus for the circulation of the social energies as well as being one of the important interpreters of the significance of those circulations.

It is interesting to note how, following the discovery of the deaths of Romeo and Juliet in both Shakespeare's play and Brooke's narrative poem, the Friar ultimately submits to the judgement of the Prince. In the play, he receives from the Prince the acknowledgement that 'We still have known thee for a holy man'. The two sources of moral and political authority – like the Emperor and the Pope, the secular and the ecclesial arms of government – affirm and support each other. They constitute the basis of the commonweal and the moderation of its dynamics. But the play depicts a new kind of commonweal in which a shift of power has been affected away from the sacramental offices of the church to the secular offices of the state. As such, the ending of the play establishes the tension between the Catholic refusal and the Protestant establishment of the secular space. One is now subordinate to the other, but a tension nevertheless is evident, for the sacramental offices of the church have been instrumental in bringing about the present peace and reconciliation. The Prince only gives judgement (and punishes) in the new situation created by the working of providence and grace, in the operation of which the Friar (as the sacerdotal arm of the church) is the central figure. The Prince ratifies what has come about, and yet nevertheless the play ends with submission of the church to a secular ruling. In his letter *To the Christian Nobility of the German Nation*, Martin Luther stated: 'I say therefore that since the temporal power is ordained of God to punish the wicked and protect the good, it should be left free to perform its office in the whole body of Christendom without restriction and without respect to persons, whether it affects the pope, bishops, priests, monks, nuns or anyone else.' The church is superseded by the state at the end of *Romeo and Juliet*, the 'religious' as it was once understood gives way to a new secularizing force, in a manner which suggests not simply the contemporary *realpolitik*, but also the fact that the tension between these powers is not resolved, only suppressed. A certain understanding of 'religion' is being depoliticized, and as we will see in the next chapter this forces a new understanding of 'religion' (as depoliticized) to emerge. A set of contraries frames the ending of the play, just as a set of contraries frames the opening of the play. The local contraries of Montague and Capulet have been dissolved into other, larger, one might say socio–metaphysical contraries: church–state, soul–body, private–public. It is a 'glooming peace' that dawns.

It is moderation of these social and therefore religious dynamics that needs to be restored. The haste with which Romeo and Juliet rush towards the consummation of their desire both continues and perpetuates the immoderation. Their haste finds wider reverberations in other hot and urgent acts, from Tybalt's aggressive demand for satisfaction from Romeo, to Mercutio's provocation of Tybalt, to Romeo's own turn upon Tybalt, to Capulet's sudden arrangement of Juliet's marriage. This series of interconnected acts brings to a fever-pitch the extremities abroad and the pace of the play. But the Friar embodies another timing, that liturgical timing which instils the Christian virtue of temperance. In the quiet retreat of his cell he upbraids Romeo for his 'wild acts' and reacts to Paris's demands for an imminent wedding with 'The time is very short'. Liturgy, which had in subtle ways dictated events earlier in the play – the 'old accustomed feast' and Juliet's birthday – now begins to dominate as order is restored. Confession and absolution, marriage, eucharistic and funeral rites will all play their part in the human submission once again to the liturgical cosmos. The Friar is the focus now for effecting a transposition of time and action – 'out of thy long-experience'd time' Juliet seeks present council – but this can only be effected through entry into death and a rising to new life. The deaths of Romeo and Juliet are necessary for the restoration of peaceful order and the transmutation of the two lovers into gilded saint-like figures. At the Friar's hand they will become a living sacrifice that will enable a new communion. This is his ultimate priestly act. 'God's bread!' exclaims Capulet to Juliet, recalling her earlier association with a lamb when he tells her to 'Graze where you will'.

The timing of the play is such that Juliet, who goes to the Friar to confess before the 'evening mass', surrenders herself to a symbolic death (a day early because of the further rashness of Capulet) at the time the priest celebrates by performing symbolically the sacrifice of Christ. It is the sacrifice of Christ that brings about the restoration of the world and his return as bridegroom to redeem his bride, the church. The eschatological fulfilment of the covenant made between God and human creatures turns upon the resurrection of the dead. Shakespeare plays upon these theological motifs with a profound and perhaps disturbing irony. Juliet, experiencing her own Gethsemane, fears the tomb and wakes 'before that time that Romeo come to redeem me'. When she 'dies' it is mockingly announced by Capulet that 'The bridegroom he is come already'. To her rescue comes the Friar, who will affirm that married by God, Juliet is a bride of Christ by a conflation of marriage and funeral

15

rites: 'Is the bride ready to go to church?' Love, death and the promised awakening consort together in complex metaphorical ways that transpose the secular and mundane in a manner which recalls another Catholic's religious vision and ironic distance bordering on parody – Donne in *The Canonization*, *The Relique* and *The Funerall*:

> Wee dye and rise the same, and prove
> Mysterious by this love.

Capulet announces over Juliet's body the epithet 'martyr'd' as time now slows on a return to the 'lasting labour of his pilgrimage'. The Friar rehearses (and again it is ironic how prophetic is his speaking) the doctrine of eternal life and the translation of Juliet to heaven. Romeo takes up the prophecy in his own life-after-death presentiments that follow the dissipation of the funereal dirge of Juliet's seeming-death begun by the musicians:

> My dreams presage some joyful news at hand.
> My bosom's lord sits lightly in his throne
> And all this day an unaccustom'd spirit
> Lifts me above the ground with cheerful thoughts.
> I dreamt my lady came and found me dead –
> Strange dream that give a dead man leave to think! –
> And breath'd such life with kisses in my lips
> That I reviv'd and was an emperor. (V.3, 85–6)

Romeo glimpses here an almost trinitarian participation – the lord upon the throne in apocalyptic fashion, the spirit stirring and elevating. And Juliet is called, as elsewhere, 'my lady', which subtly associates her with the Virgin Mary in this explicitly Christian theological framing. The dead will rise to new life, Juliet will herself 'die with a restorative'. These are the final forms of 'change . . . to the contrary', a motif which has governed the action of the play throughout. It is as if the play has become a rood screen on which is portrayed the saints beneath the sacrificial sign of Christ's crucifixion. The screen concealed and intensified the eucharistic celebration on the altar and recalled the last judgement of all things and the resurrection of the dead.

16

The final eschatological change-to-the-contrary has none of the violent, headstrong giddiness of the early pullulating extremities. With their suicides Romeo and Juliet fully internalize, that is, take upon themselves, the violences that have operated in and with and through them. They close the cycle of victims and perpetrators of violence and end the repetitions of reprisal – like scapegoats, like Christ himself who according to the church Fathers gave himself to death wilfully. In fact Donne made Christ's 'Heroique' suicide the dramatic centre-piece of a treatise on self-homicide, *Biathanatos*. Only by this final focusing of the violences can the 'purge', the 'scourge', be effected. The profane rebellion that tore apart the fabrics of the commonweal and ritual time – like the torn hymens of maids whose maidenheads are 'cut off' (I.1, 21) – enters an eschatological change, becoming part of a 'work of heaven'. Heaven draws close to earth in the final act and its coming brings confession, pardon, forgiveness and judgement ('All are punish'd'). Juliet, who Romeo saw (truly) as angel and saint, becomes exactly that; and Romeo, who Juliet pictures as a constellation of stars (a heavenly body), finally moves beyond the firmament of chance and change towards an

> everlasting rest
> And shake the yoke of inauspicious stars
> From this world-wearied flesh. (V.3, 110–12)

In shaking the yoke of inauspicious stars, the pair of star-crossed lovers transcends the stars themselves towards the sun, having effected the earthly reconciliation and facilitated the new order. Romeo remarks that Juliet's 'beauty makes / This vault a feasting presence, full of light'. We return to the intimations of their sainthood in Capulet's 'old accustomed feast'. For with the saints there is – as *The Golden Legend*, that famous book of the lives of the saints expresses it – 'the debt of interchanging neighbourhood'. The movement between the earthly and heavenly is fluid in the sacramental worldview. At the balcony scene Juliet is called the sun and exhorted to 'arise fair sun'. By the end of the play the sun, that throughout the play has in fact served to separate them, now provides a dawn that they can share.

By the Act of Uniformity of 1559 every parish was required to have a Book of Homilies that were appointed to be read on certain occasions in the year. The 'Homily Against Contention and Brawling' opens:

> This day (good Christian people) shall be declared unto you, the unprofitableness and shameful unhonesty of contention, strife and debate, to the intent, that when you shall see as it were in a table painted before your eyes, the evilfavouredness and deformity of this most detestable vice, your stomaches may be moved to rise against it, and to detest and abhor that sin, which is so much to be hated, and pernicious, and hurtful to all men.

The next sentence clarifies the focus for this injunction against civil disorder: 'But among all kinds of contention, none is more hurtful than is contention in matters of religion.' The contents of the homily that follows, the place appointed for its reading, and the minister appointed to give that reading all emphasize that obedience in matters of faith will therefore enable religion to maintain rather than threaten such good social order. What is significant for the development of my argument is that religion here is a series of practices by which the sacred and the secular are bound each to the other. Religion is piety, devotion, adoration, pilgrimage. It regulates and reaffirms certain understandings of the self and the social and their relationship to the cosmic and divine; through liturgies and sacramental offices it gives shape to time and meaning to space. The precious particularity of Romeo as Romeo and Juliet as Juliet, and their shared love, is maintained only because of the divinity that enfolds them and makes them to be much more than they are while being who they are. Love makes them wonder, and in wonder they do not so much transcend the mundane as transfigure it. That is the beauty of their first encounter at the Capulet feast. It is an incarnate spirituality that transfigures into angels, saints and worshippers the physical, sexual and social energies in which they both participate.

But the world in which they loved and in which even the 'woe' of this love can make sense – that is, effect a greater good – was slipping away. A nostalgia marks Shakespeare's recreation of this Catholic worldview which the setting in the medieval city-state of Verona allows. The redemption of time and place is a product of artifice and is never fully able to conquer the tensions it has raised and treated. Religion was changing. The public affirmation of shriving, adoration of the saints, the church as regulating lived time, the social consciences and the commonweal, evident in the play, has to be placed alongside the note struck in that 'Homily Against Contention and Brawling' – religion was no longer a matter for open discussion. And it is in this way that Shakespeare's play lies strung between an older sense of divine comedy and a more modern sense of the tragic: where the modern account of tragedy – evident from Racine and Pascal to Beckett – concerns the hiddenness or absence of the divine and the rule of the arbitrary. For the last acts of the play are attempts to maintain and distil even further the purity of Romeo and Juliet's love and the moral and theological world in which such love is valued and validated, but through the very self-conscious employment of seeming, dissimulation, concealment of intention, transgression of the law and secrecy. The subterfuge compromises everyone – including the Friar – and generates confusion and ironies that leave behind dark shadows not easily dissolved. Emblematic here is the apothecary whom Shakespeare portrays sympathetically, and yet whose condition of being poor may well be the grounds for receiving a greater punishment. Of course the Prince does not specify who will be pardoned and who punished. The Friar is pardoned; does that mean the apothecary then is to be punished? In Brooke's narrative poem the apothecary is hanged. Shakespeare suspends the judgement, but the resonance of 'present death in Mantua' does not go away. The sun does not rise upon Verona at the end of the play, even though Romeo and Juliet are embossed in gold. And the very turning of their love into an aesthetic object (and the play is also one such object) strikes discordantly. The statue suggested by the Montagues and Capulets defeats classification: is it a piece of art, an effigy or the representation of two saints ? The autocratic presence of the Prince likewise suggests an authority detached from and ready to rule with respect to the religious, moral, cosmic and liturgical order. The admission to the Capulets and Montagues that there was some 'winking at your discords' suggests a legislative power that does not always see aright; it suggests a pragmatics of power that renders ruling open to the charge of being arbitrary. These troubling dissonances Shakespeare will treat again in characters like Fortinbras in *Hamlet* and the Duke in *Measure for Measure*, but we can note that in *The Winter's Tale* 'redemption' is wrought when the 'statue' returns to life. It is as if the sacramental world Romeo, Juliet and the Friar inhabit is being preserved in amber, and yet it is in that very preservation being silenced. 'The sun for sorrow' will not reveal the way ahead.

Close to the date when the play was being written, close to the place where Shakespeare was writing, John Donne and his brother Henry were being visited by their own 'ghostly confessor'. It is difficult to believe that Shakespeare did not know of the event, since the London chronicler, John Stow, reports on it. John Carey relates the story:

> In May 1593 a young man called William Harrington was arrested in Henry Donne's rooms on suspicion of being a priest. Henry, of course, was taken into custody too. When charged, Harrington denied that he was a priest, but poor Henry, faced with torture, betrayed him. He admitted that Harrington had shriven him while he was staying in his rooms . . . Like other Catholic martyrs, he refused to be tried by a jury because he did not wish to implicate more men than necessary in the guilt of his destruction. He was condemned and, on 18 February 1594, taken out to die. In the cart, with the rope around his neck, he began to address his 'loving countrymen', only to be interrupted with insults by Topcliffe [Elizabeth's chief torturer]. But his courage did not fail, and he denounced Topcliffe from the scaffold as a 'tyrant and blook-sucker'. Like the Babington conspirators, he was dis-embowelled alive. Stow records that, after he had been hanged and cut down, he 'struggled' with the executioner who was about to use the knife on him.
>
> Henry Donne, having knowingly harboured a priest, was guilty of felony. But he did not live long enough to come to trial. Imprisoned at first in the Clink, he was moved to Newgate, where the plague was raging, and died within a few days.[5]

Romeo's 'religion' was being expunged and a new understanding of 'religion' was already emerging that we will investigate in the next chapter. What the play details and bears witness to is a tension involved in the dissolution of a certain discursive formation (that is, specific networks of practices, gestures and ways of speaking) that 'religion' was implicated in in a premodern context. Catholic beliefs and practices organize the space in which the play is produced; they organize the sociality and subjectivities represented in the play. This Catholic religious network, and the system of ideas which constructed a sacramental view of the world, was breaking up, being challenged, being transformed, being caught up in dissimulations, parodies, internalizations of violence, ironies and confusions. A certain crisis is evident which the religious worldview is trying to accommodate but cannot – for the crisis is within the religious worldview itself. From new practices came new pieties, new discursive formations giving rise to other understandings of 'religion'.

As I said at the beginning of this chapter, as the understanding of religion changes so does the understanding of related concepts, particularly the secular. In the traditional worldview the *saeculum* had no autonomous existence. In a liturgical cosmos no one and nothing remains separated from divine providence – 'all are punish'd' and all are recipients of grace. What we witness at the end of *Romeo and Juliet* is a certain tension between the sacramental world and a secular politics with respect to the government of that world. The tensions registered in the play signal a separation into two kingdoms of the sacred from the profane. The secularization processes throughout the reigns of Henry VIII, Edward VI and Elizabeth had been carried through in the name of a greater spiritualization and purification of the true faith. The Protestant radicals opposed not the Christian faith as such but abuses of the faith. Pilgrimages, the adoration of the saints, the apotropaic rather than the symbolic understanding of the sacraments (what came to be labelled superstitions and idolatries) were religious decadences that had to be scourged. This profoundly affected the liturgical understanding of the world. To abrogate holy days was to change the nature of time and the relationship between work, leisure and worship. To take over church lands, dissolve monasteries, call for the destruction of statues even of patronal saints, and forbid pilgrimages and processions, was to change the

21

nature of space and the relationship been one's home and sacred place. The mapping of holy loci, therefore the networking of sacred power, was redrawn. To rethink the sacraments and ceremonies as symbols or 'mere outward forms' (1549 Book of Common Prayer) was to transform the nature of materiality itself, rendering the natural world opaque, silent and inert. No longer was materiality caught up in the Friar's doxology: 'O, mickle is the powerful grace that lies / In plants, herbs, stones and their true qualities'. These changes to time, space and materiality affected the very body itself – its labouring, its movements, its actions, its extensions beyond itself with respect to other bodies (the gilds, the parish, the community of the saints). At the end of *Romeo and Juliet* bodies are frozen – either in death, or in proposed statuary, or in waiting for a dawn that cannot come. A new space and a new understanding of the body were emerging, a space and a body in which God's presence was only available through the eyes of faith – and faith understood as a set of doctrinal principles to be taught, a set of interpretative keys to be passed down, passed on, for one's experience in the world. The understanding of secularity itself changed as such a space began to open.

If the above can be taken as a reading of 'religion' and 'secularity' as they are operating in and through the event of *Romeo and Juliet* at a time not yet ripe enough to call 'modernity', what then is revealed to us about these terms when that cultural event of *Romeo and Juliet* is replayed in postmodernity?

Romeo and Juliet II

The violent originality of Baz Luhrmann's 1996 film version of *Romeo and Juliet* might best be appreciated if viewed alongside Franco Zeffirelli's famous production almost thirty years earlier. Zeffirelli cast two unknowns among a galaxy of well-known Hollywood actors such as Michael York and Milo O'Shea, in a film which placed great emphasis upon the innocence and inexperience of the two lovers. For example, Romeo's violent declarations of affection for Rosaline (Act 1, scene 2) are omitted. The pure, childlike nature of their love stands in tension with the overwhelming opulence of their surroundings and the knowing innuendos being bartered around them. Two contrasting aesthetics emerge: the beauty of innocence that the filming associates with the lush Italian landscape and natural elements (trees and flowers, gentle breezes and sunlight) and the cultured, sumptuous beauty of the film's production. It was shot on location in Italy and, through its framing and cinematography, attempts to recreate a city-state in the Italian Renaissance. Costume, colours, set-designs, camera angles, even poses by characters, self-consciously allude to masterpieces of Renaissance art. The camera lingers, the narrative flows inexorably towards its tragic ending, but in a leisurely manner reminiscent of a visit to an art gallery. The fresh, virginal, idealized relationship between Romeo and Juliet sets them apart from the bawdiness and stunning sensuousness of their real context, establishing a soft-focused critique of nascent capitalism and the world of the *objet d'art*. The film catches, then, something of the 1960s social critique offered by the hippy movement, Woodstock and flower-power. It ironically turns that critique into a box-office success.

The 'religious' scenes support the critique, although not entirely. The Franciscan side of Father Laurence is accentuated, though the poverty of his calling and the simplicity of his approach to life are somewhat at odds with the luxurious woollen folds of his habit. We find the same tension inside his 'cell'. The church used is austere in its colours, with white/grey walls reflecting the purity and intensity of the Italian light, but a magnificent painted crucifix hangs above the chancel steps. The church seems to mediate between the opulent wealth of the city-state and the guilelessness of a love that it solemnizes but does not quite embody. The spiritualization and naturalization of Romeo and Juliet's virginal affections are given historical religious colouring; the religious itself is not the point, just a backdrop, a staging. Zeffirelli's film is a visual expression of a lyric written by the 1960s and 1970s American folksinger Don Maclean about Vincent van Gogh's suicide: 'I could have told you Vincent / The world was never made for one as beautiful as you'. It plays out a theme familiar in Hollywood cinema at the time, of innocence and experience (cf. *The Graduate*).

Contrast this with Luhrmann's film, which is more than thirty minutes shorter and makes considerable use of jump-cuts to give pace to the narrative and provide the film with a certain jagged edge. The action and the pace run rough-shod over the poetry. There is none of Zeffirelli's reverence for Shakespeare's iambic pentameter. Shot in Mexico City, Verona is a contemporary urban landscape with its extremes of poverty and decadent wealth, its drug-taking and weapon-wielding, its disaffected (seemingly unemployed) youth and its heavy policing. There is a radical ironization of Shakespeare's opening sentiments, narrated by a newsreader as part of the headlines: 'In fair Verona (where we lay our scene)'. The ironization (and the iconoclasm it sets up) ricochets like the bullets throughout the film, heightened by the cutting, the rapid shot–reverse-shots, the panning, tracking and zooms.

Speed is of the essence and theatricality is the idiom. The broadcasting of news events on the television opens and closes the film, so that the whole narrative is portrayed as a hyped news item. The production is self-consciously theatrical – even to the point of using a stage-set ruin of an open-air theatre on the beach as a frame for several scenes (including Mercutio's Queen Mab speech). The back wall of the stage has been blown apart, so that the incoming tide is viewed through the ruined proscenium arch. The natural is a cultural creation.

As with the Bernstein/Sondheim recasting of *Romeo and Juliet* as *West Side Story*, the violent tensions are given racial colouring: the Spanish/Italian (with hints of Mafia connections) Capulets versus the white-skinned Montagues, ruled by the black chief of police (the Prince) who is the uncle of the black transvestite and drag artist Mercutio.

Irony and theatrical hype blend with elements of the camp, the macho-masculine and the sexually ambiguous. At the Capulet party Mercutio performs a dance routine in a white sequin bra and tight skirt flanked by six male dancers, Capulet capers about as the Emperor Nero in a toga of blue sequins, standing at one point on a table with the toga drawn up to show his underwear, and Lady Capulet, dressed as Cleopatra, passionately kisses Tybalt who has donned the horns of Satan and the dark suit of a 1930s gigolo. The 'old accustomed feast' has turned into a millionaire's fancy dress ball. The camera spins and focuses as it views the scene through the eyes of Romeo, dressed as a knight in shining armour, on ecstasy. The

24

visual ostentation of the film, its excess of movement and colour and sound – captured in montage shots of fireworks and a fairground Ferris wheel at night – transform the film itself into a consumer delight. It is extravagant and ephemeral, precious and kitsch and, picking up on Shakespeare's intuited association of pricks and sword, the film possesses an erotic and violent intensity.

Fetishism is pervasive. The camera adores objects – and this adoration, this worship, has analogues with the dramatic heightening of the Catholic religion. Tybalt's shoes, the handling of guns, Juliet's ring, clothing that draws attention to itself or to the bodies of those who wear it, bullets, tablets, vials of coloured liquid, cars, tropical fish, ornamental decor – all become endowed with dramatic and magical allure. Of course, there are elements of this fetishism in Shakespeare's play itself, where attention is given to significant stage props, but in Luhrmann's world everything is a stage prop. All objects are given an aesthetic status that, in the context of the Catholicism, turns the visual experience into a form of idolatry. Each object announces that it has been chosen to play a part in the cinematic production, so that nothing is ordinary, nothing is allowed to be just background. Everything is self-consciously 'produced'; everything is a special effect.

It is not only objects that are fetishized: it is scenes themselves, cinema itself. Like many of Shakespeare's plays, *Romeo and Juliet* has its famous set-pieces, scenes that theatrical history has turned into points where the audience's attention is pre-focused. There is Hamlet's 'To be or not to be' speech, there is Lear on the heath, there is Titania's infatuation with Bottom and Macbeth's banquet when the ghost of Banquo appears. In *Romeo and Juliet* there is the balcony scene. Tourists in Verona can be shown a balcony where they are told Romeo first exchanged his vows with Juliet. Luhrmann's balcony scene is a theatrical set-piece trumpeting itself as such. Its ingeniousness is extravagant. Zeffirelli's balcony scene could have been staged in a theatre and caught on camera. Luhrmann's balcony scene is pure cinematography. The transformation of medium (from stage to film set) is signalled in the move from air to water, from balcony to swimming pool, from the night to the fluorescence of underwater illumination. As Leonardo diCaprio and Claire Danes circle about each other, twisting and turning in an underwater embrace, what is spoken (the content of the action) issues from beneath what is shot and how it is shot. What is conveyed is the enchantment, the alchemy, of cinematography. The significance and value of the image lie less in terms of what is *being* imaged, than in the composition of the image itself. This has the effect of trans-figuring the nature of what is being filmed – turning the scene itself into an aesthetic and erotically pleasing object. It is not an object desired for its own sake, but desired because, in being rendered desirable (by the camera), it makes us desire it. Immersed in the sounds of water, human voices exchanging intimacies, and a light piano music, we are invited to enjoy our own desiring. We forget this is Shakespeare's *Romeo and Juliet* (the dialogue has been radically cut), we no longer desire to see performed for us Shakespeare's *Romeo and Juliet* – what we desire is the continuation of this spectacular production, we desire the prolongation of the allure of the image as image. What is found breathtaking, what is aesthetically experienced, is not the Shakespeare but the spectacular itself, which comes by way of the commodification of both Shakespeare and the history of the transmission of his work. In his next film, *Moulin Rouge*, Luhrmann has the plot revolve around a musical extravaganza entitled 'Spec-tacular, Spectacular'. The special effects become – as Juliet whispers to Romeo – 'the god of my idolatry'.

This pervasive fetishism in which objects have aura, and the idolatrous culture it invokes, give the film a quality that is a distinct-ive hallmark of Luhrmann's work. *William Shakespeare's Romeo & Juliet* is the second in a trio (*Strictly Ballroom* was the first and *Moulin Rouge* the third) of what Luhrmann calls his Red Curtain phase. Each film situates a dramatic, even sincerely sought, relationship in an irreality. Let me explain what I mean by that, for it is the manner in which religion is rendered an aspect of that irreality which is a significant indicator of the role religion is playing in postmodernity. Again, a comparative contrast with Zeffirelli's film is useful. As I have pointed out, Zeffirelli attempts to recreate the authentic life-style of an Italian Renaissance city. Historical accuracy is important in conveying a sense of the historical past. The play is underwritten, then, by a certain realist appeal; a certain state of things as they once were and which can be replicated by returning to actual Italian locations and filling the sites with people dressed in researched

26

costumes, bearing researched stage props, and acting in ways appropriate to that period. Renaissance music and dancing are performed at the Capulet feast, for example. Zeffirelli wants to make the plot of *Romeo and Juliet* credible for the contemporary audience by means of the realism of the setting. The camera *records* this detailed reproduction. Luhrmann's world refuses this photographic realism, but it refuses also a surrealism; that is, the film is not dream-like, nor does it attempt to depict the realms of the unconscious. Luhrmann's world is more hallucinogenic: what is recorded as 'out there', composing the nature of things and actions in the world, is bent continually by the way it is perceived or received. The camera mimics the actors in the scene, adrenalin-rushed and narcotically heightened. People, objects and events are excessive to their material condition, such that what is real is forever in question. Frequently, Luhrmann films *through* other media – mirrors, a curtained window, a fish-tank, a drugged state of mind, water. Things never just appear as such; their appearance is always produced – in fact, overproduced. This is what I term the irreality of the film. The French sociologist Jean Baudrillard might term this 'hyperreality'. In 1981 in his provocative book *Simulacra and Simulation* he writes of the 'loss of communication' that both produces or is produced by the 'escalation of simulacrum', such that there is a 'hyperreality of communication and of meaning. More real than the real, that is how the real is abolished.'[6] With irreality, reality *is* a special effect; and as such it is always and only virtual.

The role religion plays in the creation of this effect is emphatic in Luhrmann's film. In fact, one could say that the Roman Catholic church is its main character and sacramentalism the film's dominant theme. In the opening montage of shots a huge statue of Christ atop a church is circled, spliced with close-ups of his face. In a zoom-out shot the tower blocks of Capulet and Montague stand either side of the figure. Civil strife is focused on the mediating figure of the Christian church. Christ stands with his arms open in welcome to both sides of the quarrel. When we descend to the violence played out on the street between rival gangs at a petrol station, the religious theme is picked up quickly: a nun ushers some convent girls into a bus while the Montagues make lascivious gestures towards them; Abba Capulet opens his mouth to show that his front teeth have

27

been replaced with a metal plate on which the word 'sin' is scratched; a crucifix dangles like a charm from Benvolio's gun and when Tybalt invites Benvolio to look upon his death, he opens his jacket to reveal a t-shirt with an image of Christ printed on it in lurid colours. Of course, this is symbolic over-kill and that is the point.

Religious excess is prevalent throughout the film, from the collection of images of the Virgin Mary, saints and angels and the array of votive candles in Juliet's bedroom, to the tattoo of the cross that covers Friar Laurence's back; from the choirs in the church and the images of the sacred heart to the huge canvas of Mary on the staircase of the Capulet mansion. The ultimate expression of this devotional excess is the deathbed scene itself. Romeo locks himself into the echoing spaces of the church. Through a crack in the door he views the nave. The approach to the high altar is flanked by rows of blue-neon crucifixes, flowers, and lamps fashioned like glowing tapers. As we slowly track towards the centre of the church the altar has been replaced by a catafalque–cum–bed on which Juliet lies, surrounded by a baroque fantasy of candles and statuary. Sex and death are indistinguishable; the bed is the altar on which the two lovers will offer themselves eucharistically. Death is the consummation, the final celebration of an aesthetic ecstasy; as death is the consummation in *Moulin Rouge* of 'Spectacular, Spectacular'. The film is emphatic that Romeo and Juliet *take* their lives; that they are forced towards an excessive gesture by the heightened emotions, the evident indulgences and violences around them.

The film's irreality is an expression and extension of this religious world in which the two families live. It is not a world issuing from Shakespeare's poetry; it is rather an elaborate staging for the poetry. The priestly role of the Franciscan is reduced to a perfunctory office. Though the performance by Pete Postlethwaite is colourful, even erotic, we rarely see him dressed liturgically. The action issues not from the play-as-liturgy as from a certain emotional and cultural distemper that the church both figures and transcends. For despite its kitsch attachment to holy accessories and paraphernalia (the baroque is an aesthetic forerunner of the kitsch), there are moments when the transcendent is taken more seriously, when we view the action from above, from the head of Christ. There are moments of devotional awe and reverence relating both to what the lovers feel for each other and to Christ's own love. These moments run counter to the iconoclasm which sometimes borders on the blasphemous (lending an added *frisson* to the film). The tone of the film's portrayal of Roman Catholicism is ambivalent and irreducibly so.

Luhrmann seems to want to explore what possibilities remain for genuine relationships that can transcend the cultural conditions of postmodernity; whether 'genuine' can ever be used as a descriptive term again. Religion figures in those possibilities, in terms of a distinctive and particular piety. The deathbed scene points to the inability to escape the excess superficialities which decadent attention to 'staging' brings, yet before each kills themselves they glance up like martyrs to the heavens. But there remains an inability to gain any moral high ground, any perspective that can change the situation. When Juliet shoots herself we view the scene twice: once from her level and once from above, from the Christic perspective. Even so the elevated perspective only permits a certain pity. It achieves not a transcendence but only a distance that betrays an inability to change the situation below, or to intervene. The only transcendence is experience of the spectacular itself; a cheap, commercial transcendence that undermines any potential for tragedy in what happens to Romeo and Juliet. We have enjoyed the spectacle too much. As an audience we are drawn into the rhythms and the riots of colour and shot. We not only accept the excess; we feast upon the visual extravagance that is filtered through a tasteless yet gilded Roman Catholicism. We too are seduced, hooked, stimulated, doused in the sensuous music, and rendered incapable of either laying the blame or feeling guilty. We leave the lovers on their bed, the camera floats above them turning the scene below into an image of a constellation above, the classical music draws to a sweet finale, and we flashback nostalgically over the high points of their affection. Romeo and Juliet are already a romantic memory – the raw emotion quickly disappearing into the rich and clichéd surfaces captured on celluloid.

We are distanced quickly from the action or what it might mean. When we return to the world outside the church, the colour has been filtered from the film and a grey and grainy texture imposes a new alienation. The closing scene takes from the original play the most minimal of lines. The chief of police screams that all are punished and underlines 'That heaven finds mean to kill your joys with love', but no one else speaks and there is little sense of punishment for the parents, since the relationships between each child and their family has been estranged and strained throughout. There is no sense of contrition or reconciliation and the Friar is missing. There is no sense of the restoration of civic and/or moral order, only a cessation of violence that seems, at best, temporary. The aggressive policing remains; its very aggression symptomatic of a defensiveness, a need to protect. The events seem not to close, but rather to withdraw, and the emotional disengagement is completed when the audience get up to leave the cinema. From the scene on the steps of the church we cut to the newsreader again and the television screen framing the events. The drama becomes one more 'story' of urban 'woe' reported that evening. The camera pulls out from the screen so that the words and image increasingly retreat into a darkness surrounding the set. If the film is watched on video then screen frames screen: we have been entertained and the entertainment has concluded. The final withdrawal is the retreat from movies and media themselves – but towards what? Only the flickering background darkness of an otherwise empty studio.

This self-conscious staging fuses media with religious hype, just as the transcendent, Christic perspective is also a Skycam and an overhead tracking shot. The camera is god-like in its fashioning, framing and in its all-seeing. As such the religious cannot be separated from the theatrical, the cinematic and the aesthetic. I pointed out earlier the ways in which Shakespearian theatre overflowed into the public and religious domains, just as these domains overflowed into the theatrical world. I drew attention to the circulation of social energies. But in Luhrmann's world it is not that the cinematic and the religious influence each other, so much as they cannot be discerned to be at all distinct – both mediate, both fetishize, both transcend the human comedy, and both bestow a melodramatic attention on the sign. For both, the content (Catholic doctrine and Shakespeare's play) takes second place to its presentation; and for both a world is created which constantly displaces and frustrates positivist or realist handlings of it. The irony, the play, the excess, the ambiguity, the overcoding are irreducible – and it is this very irreducibility that demands and articulates the assimilation of the religious with a camp

30

aesthetic. Religion is cultural production and nothing more. The religious worldview does not announce a *sacramentum mundi*, a moral ordering, an affirmation of the transcendental significance of each person, act and object. Instead of the liturgical time of confession and mass, the merging of the ecclesial with the seasonal calendar, the jump-cuts accentuate the more general collapse of time to the 'now', the moment of optimal intensity. Luhrmann's production portrays a profound loss of the sacramental in exactly the sites where one might hope it could be found. But the film is not concerned with the possibilities for its restoration. Neither does the ending of the film capture the tensions of whether such a restoration is possible. The film questions order itself, questions power, questions authority as it questions authenticity. The agonistic and arbitrary nature of power in Luhrmann's world is not judged by the practices of piety nor shaped by the liturgical cosmos. If the events are at all controlled from above, the star-crossed lovers are the victims of a dark unknowing fatality. The destiny theme of the play, for example, turns, for Luhrmann, upon Mercutio's dying curse: 'A plague a' both your houses!' The chromium-blue sky now becomes bruised and foreboding. This staging of fortune turns destiny into a power no less arbitrary than the chief of police's. For given that Mercutio picked the fight with Tybalt in the heat of a febrile madness, fortune's entrance is not as an agent of the good, the just and the true. Hence, Luhrmann's film finally withdraws into its own irreality rather than resolves the conflict between Capulet and Montague; for the conflictual itself is the transcendental principle.

Unlike Zeffirelli's production, Luhrmann, while drawing some associations between Juliet's virginity and the Virgin Mary's, views neither Romeo nor Juliet as innocent of conflict. Romeo can be as distempered as any of the other young men. Luhrmann includes the bawdy conversation between Benvolio and Romeo about Rosaline, and while allowing Romeo moments of Hamlet-like self-reflection the violence of his own emotions is never forgotten. There are moments when Juliet plays in turn the innocent and the sexually knowing. She can also irrupt into tantrums of her own. She is no coy child on the edge of womanhood. Their loving shares a violence towards each other comparable to the violence between the rival gangs. Their self-murder then does not expiate the more general violence but constitutes one more violent act. Their suicide lacks sacramental significance and so it cannot effect a sacramental operation, while staging itself sacramentally – with Juliet's bed as the altar upon which their love is ultimately consummated. The suicide dresses itself dramatically in kitsch sacramental garb. Any economy of grace, translating the taking of their lives into the offering of their lives – suicide becoming sacrifice – is absent. And so the film does not end as it began, with freeze frames of the Christ figure opening his arms in a gesture of peace to the cityscape below. Nor does it end with the final transfiguration of Romeo and Juliet into statues of pure gold. The two covered bodies are wheeled out of the church on stretchers and into waiting ambulances. There is no sense of resurrection here.

Religion is not a word used in the film at all. The early scene in Shakespeare's play when Romeo employs the word in conversation with Benvolio (Act 1, scene 2) is cut. Nevertheless, as I have shown, religion permeates the whole production such that the city of Verona offers no secular, civic space. The Prince as chief of police accentuates the frenetic and intoxicating pace of the action. A cliché of Hollywood hard-action cop movies, he is closely associated with movement – fast emergency cars, surveillancing helicopters. He breaks into a scene and leaves it just as rapidly. He offers no sense of a stable civic order, distinct from and unembroiled with the dramatic devotional practices of the Catholic faith. Luhrmann's world is not a secular world. And yet, as I have also suggested, it is not a surreal world or a real world either. The world is irreal – mythologized and yet shallow. As we will see in chapter 4, postmodern religion can employ a magic realism of various kinds, from Salman Rushdie's *Satanic Verses* to Philip Pullman's *Dark Materials* trilogy, to Kevin Smith's film *Dogma*. The supernatural comes from the other side of C. S. Lewis's wardrobe and enters the house, garden and urban landscape itself. But the supernatural is lofty and impersonal in its presence, not close to hand and down right ordinary. It figures a certain aporia, an unnameable, operating powerfully in, through and beyond the conspicuous consumption that makes the material order so over-inflated and superficial. It is as if religion remains – in the accoutrement of Roman Catholic devotions – but it has been eviscerated, turned into gaudy and tawdry surfaces. Religion no longer names that which brings about the star-crossed destiny of the main characters – and yet the shell of what was once religion serves still to figure forth a burden of transcendence pressing upon the material. There is a crisis here. The film not only marks that crisis but also situates itself with respect to it. The crisis is in trying to represent at all. The film is symptomatic, for it participates in a crisis with respect to representation itself. A certain loss of confidence is evident which the film articulates – who represents, on behalf of whom? What is represented and who decides? One might say that the real itself gets lost in the politics of the real. Certainly a number of postmodern thinkers – the French sociologist Jean Baudrillard and political scientist Paul Virilio in particular – bear witness to reality as a rhetorical effect, a performance. Computer-simulated realities – and cinematography is becoming increasingly dependent upon these realities, relying upon digitalized images or computer-enhanced perception for its special effects – are only a further expression of what Virilio describes as 'the relative fusion/confusion of the factual (or operational, if you prefer) and the virtual; the ascendency of the "reality effect" over the reality principle'.[7] The optical and the cinematic become indistinguishable; representation *is* media presentation. Luhrmann's film of *Romeo and Juliet* articulates this loss of the real, this loss of confidence in whether there is anything beyond constructions and effects of the real. Luhrmann does not always view the losses pessimistically (as Baudrillard and Virilio do). A new playfulness becomes possible, a new *commedia dell'arte* appears; new forms of baroque (or elsewhere gothic) fantasy can be explored. But the question I am posing is what cultural role does religion play with respect to this 'ascendency of the "reality effect" over the reality principle'? Does it confirm, critique, validate, act as a nostalgic retreat from or perform a counter-statement to what Virilio terms 'synthetic illusion'? Furthermore, what future is suggested for religion when it comes to play such roles?

These questions cannot be adequately answered without understanding what postmodernity is both reacting against and also developing. That is, we need to appreciate the relationship between modernity, secularity, religion and theology. In this chapter I have simply wished to present the contrasting cultural roles religion is playing in these two performances of *Romeo and Juliet*. I observed

33

with respect to the late sixteenth century that social energies were already moulding a new understanding of religion; a shift was under-way. What is observed in Luhrmann's cinematic production of the play four hundred years later is the working out of the logic of those transformations. My claim here is that the role religion plays in postmodernity is the *final* working out and that we are already beginning to enter another radical transformation in the understanding of what religion means. In the 1960s Wilfred Cantwell Smith had already pronounced the concept of religion to be bankrupt. In the 1990s Nicholas Lash proclaimed religion to be at an end. As we have seen with Luhrmann, the end does not signal the falling into disuse or the oblivion of the religious. Rather, it signals exactly the opposite: the extension and hype of the religious as the ultimate vision of the excessive and the transgressive. We need to ask what this suggests about the culture of globalism and what does this bode. We need to understand the logic it is bringing to a culmination.

2

True Religion and Temporal Goods

The urge for the absolute conceived as material excess is not just a postmodern phenomenon. It has governed the legends and dreaming of generations, producing realms like Cathay, Cipango, Brazil and El Dorado. Decadence has a history, and a history intimately related to shifting understandings of the term 'religion'. The aesthetics of the kitsch and the sublime have religious heritages that return us to the dawn of modernity and the early waves of a nascent globalism. In this chapter and the next we will trace the cultural logic that leads from Shakespeare's play to Luhrmann's film.

At the Edges of the New World

We begin in early August 1492, with Columbus ready to set sail with his three ships for the West Indies. As several of his biographers have noted, 'Columbus is above all the figure with whom the Modern Age . . . properly begins'.[1] The vaulting ambition and imagination that Dante both admired and condemned in Ulysses, is respected and praised by most who write about Columbus. A different conception of being human is evident: Dante indicts Ulysses for the sin of hubris, but the Franciscan friends of Columbus extol him as a man of vision. Both hubris and vision are religious categories. Columbus opens the prologue to his journal of the discovery of America by reminding Ferdinand and Isabella of Spain of their dual acts of extending the Christian faith (by driving out the Moors) and purifying it (by expelling the Jews). He continues:

> In the same month, on the information which I had given Your Majesties about the lands of India and a ruler known as the Great Khan [which means in Spanish 'King of Kings'], of whom I told you that he, like his predecessors, had many times appealed to Rome for men learned in the Holy Faith to instruct him, an appeal to which the Holy Father had not yet responded, and about the many peoples who were being lost through belief in idolatries and the acceptance of religions of damnation, Your Majesties, being Catholic Christians and rulers devoted to the Holy Christian Faith and dedicated to its expansion and to combating the religion of Mahomet and all the idolatries and heresies, decided to send me, Christopher Columbus, to those lands of India to meet their rulers and to see the towns and lands and their distribution, and all other things, and to find out in what manner they might be converted to our Holy Faith.

Let me draw out two points of interest and significance about this prologue for a genealogy of religion. First, the pursuit of untold wealth (worldly goods) is inseparable from a missionary zeal (for the spiritual good). The beginnings of a world system in trade goes hand in glove with Christian expansion. The secular is not divorced from the sacred; in fact the sacred lends the secular endeavour its genuine telos. On 26 December Columbus, dreaming of 'a great barrel of gold', a gold mine and endless spices, reminds the King and Queen of Spain that the quantities he will bring back to Castile 'will be able to make your preparations to go to recover the Holy Sepulchre, for Your Majesties may remember my request to you that all proceeds of this voyage of mine should be used for the conquest of Jerusalem'. Each day on board ship began with a benediction, ended with the *Salve Regina* and the hours in between were divided up according to the liturgical times of terce, vespers and compline. The very voyage itself was only possible because of the persuasive powers of important churchmen: the Franciscan confessor to Queen Isabella, the Franciscan astronomer Antonio

Marchena, and the royal tutor Diego de Deza who was later Archbishop of Seville. But what is also significant is that when Bartolome de las Casas, one of the earliest colonizers of Cuba who became a Dominican Friar and Bishop of Chiapas, wrote his *Historia de las Indias* (some fifty years later), the dual motivations for the conquest of the New World came under critical scrutiny. With hindsight and his own experience of fighting on behalf of the exploited American Indians, he was sceptical of Columbus's intentions and sarcastic about the evident pursuit for gold that is a recurring theme throughout the journal. If we credit Columbus, as most of his biographers do, with much more integrity than de la Casas allows, then what we observe in *Historia de las Indias* is a shift in worldview following the great wealth which transformed the economies of Renaissance Europe and the experiences of the colonists and colonized. A secular world abounding in the confidence of new money, new greeds, new entrepreneurial opportunities, and new intellectual possibilities is becoming unhinged from the sacred and liturgical cosmos.

The second point of interest and significance about Columbus's prologue concerns the use of 'religion', 'belief' and 'faith'. Religion as the practice of piety with respect to the divine, allows for the recognition that there is 'the religion of Mahomet' and 'religions of damnation'. There is 'our Holy Faith' as distinct from 'their' 'belief in idolatries'. What is evident is that there are 'religions' (in the plural), that these concern specific beliefs and practices and that Christian faith is the benchmark for true religion. The coming of the true religion shows up the idolatrous practices of other pieties such that they become 'heresies', corrupt forms of orthodoxy. This was already an idea in the seventh century when John Damascene in his book *The Fount of Knowledge* included Judaism and Islam under a section that gave accounts of various (other) Christian heresies. But what is new is a sense of 'religion' as naming something universal, as constituting a genus that includes various species of which Christianity is the true and ideal cultic expression.

Eighteen years prior to Columbus's journal the Italian philosopher and theologian Marcilio Ficino had spelt out such an understanding of 'religion' in a remarkable and widely disseminated treatise *De Christiana Religione* and Book 14 (chapter 9) of his *Theologica Platonica*. Ficino makes explicit what seems to linger behind Columbus's understanding of 'religion' and his mission to bring what he will call 'the Holy Religion of Christianity' to the Indians. That is, that 'religion' is an innate and natural characteristic of being human. Developing an Augustinian and Thomistic understanding of human beings made in the image of God, through a revival of Platonic thinking, Ficino can claim that that which is uniquely human is the ability to contemplate what is divine and therefore 'The worship of God is as natural to human beings, as is neighing to horses or barking to dogs'.

The territorial expansion of Christianity is paralleled by the conceptual expansion of 'religion'; the new establishment of a world trading system and the new search to define the essence of religion are culturally interrelated. The correlation between geographic expansion and ideological universalism is endemic to Christianity, and it is plain that what is being defined as 'religion' and being disseminated is Christianity. At the end of Matthew's Gospel the risen Jesus makes the following proclamation: 'All authority in heaven and on earth has been given to me. Therefore go and make disciples of all nations, baptising them in the name of the Father and of the Son and of the Holy Spirit' (Matthew 28.18–19). It is one of the foundational texts for Christian missiology. The ending of the two other synoptic gospels – Mark and Luke – contain similar but not so elaborate statements. (Scholars recognize that the last nine verses of Mark's Gospel are not found in earlier and more reliable manuscripts.) What Matthew's statement evidences is a major theological transposition effected by the coming of the Christ: the transposition from the ethnic specificities of Judaism to the universalism of the Christ through the liturgical practice of baptism in the name of the trinitarian God. The Jewish Messiah pointed Judaism towards its global horizons. The writer of Luke's Gospel dramatizes this theological cataclysm and the dissemination it effected: 'repentance and forgiveness of sins will be preached in his name to all nations, beginning at Jerusalem' (Luke 24.47). Jerusalem, which had gathered together Jewish people from all over the known world for the Passover (when the Christ was crucified), would be the centre of the new cosmic reorganization. The writer of Luke's Gospel, in his Acts of the Apostles, narrates how the falling of Christ's Spirit upon the disciples – the anointing which authorized and empowered them to preach the gospel – came during the Feast of Tabernacles when 'Parthians, Medes and Elamites; residents of Mesopotamia, Judea and Cappadocia, Pontus and Asia, Phrygia and Pamphylia, Egypt and the parts of Libya near Cyrene; visitors from Rome (both Jews and converts to Judaism); Cretans and Arabs' (Acts 2.9–11) were all assembled in Jerusalem once more. Peter preached and 'three thousand were added to their number that day' (Acts 2.41). The global mission in the name of a universalist salvation had begun.

What facilitates this relationship between globalism and the dissemination of the Christian religion is technology. In his sermon to the Honorable Company of the Virginian Plantation, the technically minded John Donne puts this in terms of God's unfolding providence: 'So *God* taught us to make Ships, not to transport our selves, but to transport him'. Columbus's journal draws attention to human dependence upon technical prostheses: the quadrant, the compass, the astrolab, the ships themselves. A new form of power is evident: technological knowledge, instrumental reasoning. A transferral of power is also evident in the move from knowledge of spiritual things to knowledge of temporal things. The spiritual conquest is dependent upon the technological one, and under the aegis of that dependence new forms of authority arise. Columbus's entry for 12 November reads:

> I thought it a good idea to take some of the people from the river to convey them to Your Majesties, so that they may learn our language and tell us what there is in their country, and learn our customs and matters of the Faith, and interpret for our people when they return, for I see from my own observations that these people have no religion, nor are they idolators. They are gentle, and do not know the meaning of evil, nor killing, nor taking prisoners; they have no weapons and are so timid that one of our men can frighten away a hundred of them, just as a joke. They are ready to believe; they acknowledge that there is a God in Heaven, and are convinced that that is where we have come from, and they are quick to recite any prayer we tell them to say, and to make the sign of the cross.

39

The entry continues to show the openness of the people for con-version and slides effortlessly from this spiritual conquest, into the great domains of the geographical conquest and, finally, the enorm-ous wealth ('quantities of gold . . . thick bands of it, and there are also precious stones and pearls and endless spices') of the economic conquest. But it is the manner in which the myths of Eden and Cathay combine that is interesting. In a double exposure, two visions of paradise are superimposed upon each other: the one of paradise, where the people live in the innocence, generosity, joy and gentle-ness of their natural condition (Columbus repeatedly speaks of their nakedness, the astonishing natural beauty which surrounds them, and once even describes how they 'love their neighbours as them-selves'); the other of a material heaven furnished with never-ending supplies of precious metals and stone (like the heavenly Jerusalem in the Book of Revelation). The first vision is moral and spiritual; the second is cultural and economic. Together they suggest that material wealth is a physical expression of divine presence. Both are indicative of the aspirations of Renaissance Europe; they are projections of what it lacks and what it feels will make good that lack. There is the aspira-tion towards a new guilelessness, the moral purity that has been the legacy of Christian teaching of avoiding evil and loving one's neigh-bour. There is the aspiration towards the material heaven of excess-ive wealth, undreamt of consumption and the means for producing the most spectacular displays of power and majesty – to make out of kingship a Kings of Kings. The Great Khan of Cathay legend was supposedly a translation of the Christic title 'King of Kings'.

Man can become whatever he determines to become – this is the new note of confidence sounding at the opening of modernity. 'He [man (*sic*)] is a more reverend divinity vested with human flesh . . . [W]e can become what we will', Pico della Mirandolla wrote in 1487. At that time Mirandolla was condemned by the church for such a notion of humanity, but in the autumn of 1492, as Columbus was still crossing the great stretches of the uncharted Atlantic, Mirandolla had been pardoned. Those who acquired and founded kingdoms in the past 'owed nothing to fortune but the opportunity which gave them matter to be shaped into what form they thought fit', Niccolò Machiavelli wrote in 1513. Machiavelli's view of human beings made them more rapacious than angelic, but

Mirandolla and Machiavelli shared the same understanding of the place of human will. And Columbus epitomizes the self-made man driven by the same passion to acquire, to accumulate and to display. Following his last voyage, Columbus noted: 'Gold is most excellent . . . whoever has it may do what he wishes in the world'. This drive to conquer and claim demonstrates a shifting of power and resources from the papacy to the secular domain. It is, quite frankly, a lust for the material compounded with a desire to return to the innocence of Eden. The desire for Eden is erotically charged – by the naked abandonment of the Indians, whose bodies he describes with voyeuristic wonder. In fact, nakedness becomes the most unstable feature of the intersected projection of these two aspirations. For it is the point where the prelapsarian condition of these people is subjected to the postlapsarian interests of those who are claiming rights over them.

In this complex description and projection a contrast emerges between 'the Faith' and a people who 'have no religion'. While being without religion does not mean, for Columbus, that these people are without notions of God, or Heaven, being without religion does mean that unlike any other group of people known in Christendom, these fell outside the categories of infidel (unfaithful one) and heretic. They were neither Jews, Moors nor Manichees. They stood prior to idolatry, representing what will later be termed – developing Ficino's line of thought – 'natural religion': a state of innocence, *tabula rasa*, unused pieces of wax naturally prepared for receiving the impress of 'custom' and 'matters of the Faith'. The cultured maturity of Renaissance experience, its superiority, is constructed in and through Columbus's description of the innocence and childlike generosity of these people. The erotic interest in their nakedness and virginal state, often focusing on their private parts, uncovered breasts or minimal clothing, is turned into a paternal care for their subsequent civilizing. This is paradise, but it requires schooling. The 'Holy Religion of Christianity' is composed of 'matters' which can be taught, and imitation even without understanding ('they are quick to recite any prayer we tell them to say, and to make the sign of the cross') is taken as readiness 'to believe'. In fact, in one description of an encounter with the Indians, Columbus states: 'I look upon them already as Christians' simply because they

41

are 'subjects of Your Majesties'. It is at this very point where another new development appears as complicit with a new understanding of 'religion': the development of the nation-state. The rise of the nation-state and the authority of the secular prince are at the expense of the erosion of ecclesial power.

The Severed Bodies of the Old World

Ferdinand and Isabella laid the geographical foundations for a united Spain, but in their expulsion of the Jews, following their conquest of the Moors, an expansion of Christendom was also sought. Machiavelli called Ferdinand 'the first king in Christendom'. The king and queen spread the maps of their new Iberian kingdom before the pope whose treasury had provided them with money for the campaign. They received back a temporal mandate to govern them. Religion was recognized as a necessary political force for gaining and maintaining geographical unity. But Machiavelli hints that 'under the *pretext* of religion' (my italics) Ferdinand and Isabella became esteemed. Temporal power was detaching itself increasingly from spiritual authority. Kingdoms united by what Machiavelli listed as 'language, laws and customs' came under the rule of those who concerned themselves with 'matters of state'. Concern with matters of state demanded a new pragmatics distinct from the pursuit of heaven and the practices of piety that disciplined desire in accord with the good, the just, the true and the beautiful. 'A man who wishes to make a profession of goodness in everything must necessarily come to grief among so many who are not good. Therefore it is necessary for a Prince, who wishes to maintain himself, to learn how not to be good, and to use this knowledge and not to use it, according to the necessity of the case', Machiavelli advised.

In the detachment of the temporal from the spiritual lies the birth of modern secularism. Its historical and concrete manifestation took the form of a civil government's control of church appointments and revenues. Ferdinand and Isabella gradually gained that control, the French monarchy was granted that control in the Concordat of Bologna in 1516 and Henry VIII seized that control in the 1534 Act of Supremacy that declared that he alone was head of the church in

England. New investments in the human capacity to shape, mould and bend the old religious world order in accordance with the will to master and determine concurrently gave birth to the modern man, the man of reason, the man at the centre of a developing humanism, the man with rights set out much later by Thomas Paine and the constitutions of France and America, the man who opened another era in the history of patriarchalism. The autonomy of the sovereign prince advocated by Machiavelli and the autonomy of the emerging nation-state were autonomies to be imitated by everyone. An analogical sovereignty closely associated them, the logic of which led to the social atomism evident in the man-as-an-island parable of *Robinson Crusoe*, as we will see. The individualism of a new subject was being fashioned while the concept of religion was becoming universal and generic. In this cultural shift the practices of piety were also being refashioned: the sanctities and potencies of the church were devolving onto the divinity of kings.

In 1603 as James VI of Scotland prepared to take up the English throne he published a treatise entitled *Basilikon Doron*. As a book of instructions to a Prince (his son Henry who died in 1612), it was Machiavelli's *Il Principe* for a new generation. The treatise was prefaced by a sonnet exhorting each person to

> be stedfast, true, and plaine,
> Repress the proud, maintaining aye the right,
> Walke alwaies so, as ever in his sight,
> Who guards the godly, plaguing the prophane:
> And so ye shall in Princely vertues shine,
> Resembling right your mightie King Divine.

The 'his' in 'his sight' is purposefully ambiguous. It refers to God but also to the king – the line between the two is becoming blurred. If, in the old world order, it was the sacrament of the eucharist administered and interpreted by the church that was the focus for the material presence of God on earth, then, in the new world order, the monarch was the new focus for God's sacramental presence. The monarch replaced the mass, the body of Christ becoming the body of the king, and in this transposition was forged a new understanding of communion in terms of commonwealth.

In England this substitution had begun under Elizabeth who, having banned the procession of Corpus Christi with the monstrance bearing the body of Christ held high, initiated a series of royal tours and visits in which the spectacular extravagance of the court took to the streets. Albion's queen was created for national worship. With James I the court became the site for an elaborate appropriation of liturgy no longer possible in the churches because of the various reformation strippings. *Basilikon Doron* means 'royal or princely gift'. The gift is from God to the people. Throughout the writing, although parallels between the king and Christ are not explicit, the parallels between the biblical King David (prototype of Christ) and King James are. Christic echoes resound: like Christ, the king 'must be of no surname nor kinne'; like Christ, the king must teach by example ('for people are naturally inclined to counterfaite (like apes) their Princes maners'); and like the Christ of the final judgement, 'the Throne ye sit on is Gods'. Apostolic succession is replaced by royal lineage, for 'vertue' (an active word close to 'grace' in James's vocabulary, for 'God is the authour of all vertue') 'followeth oftest noble blood' and 'the estate royal . . . would ever be kept *sacrosanctum & extra commercium*.' Henry Peacham lavishly illustrated the treatise and turned it into an emblem book which played on the relationship between 'ikon' and 'basilikon'. As Francis Quarles wrote in the introduction to what has become the most famous book of emblems, 'An Emblem is but a silent Parable . . . Before the Knowledge of Letters, God was known by *Hieroglyphics*.' The king was, then, a national icon.

As icon the king had two bodies: he was both himself (physically) and his nation (metonymically). As the body of the nation he was also 'mixed, betwixt the Ecclesiasticall and the civill estate'. He incarnated a divine office; like Christ in John's Gospel he was the sent-one. '[A] King is not *mere laicus*', James pronounced. The focus for this new sacrality became the Banqueting House at Whitehall, designed by Inigo Jones and completed in 1622. Its very name bears biblical allusions to Solomon's temple (in the Song of Songs the bride speaks of the king taking her 'to his banqueting house and his banner over me was love') and the upper room in which Christ held his Last Supper. Here, beneath a ceiling designed by Rubens which developed Peacham's iconography in *Basilikon Doron*, were staged the famous courtly masques of the Stuart kings. These 'formed the secular counterpart to the cult of religious images'.[2] The masques were not just a representation of the king's transcendent 'vertues'; they were powerful enactments of them. They were ritualistic ceremonies involving the participation of the invited courtiers. On entering the hall the court passed into a kingdom of symbols and allegories, mythologies and hermetic signs which were the 'key' for reading the world outside, particularly the relationship between the king and the commonwealth. Here the true forms of things were revealed – for the initiated. The king was portrayed as the source of light and harmony, the font of grace and earthly beauty. His presence in the court, seated beneath an ornate baldachin (a form of ecclesial architecture framing the high altar upon which the host was consecrated), gave colour and form to the world around him. 'God brought man into the world, as the King goes in state, Lords, and earles, and persons of other ranks before him. So God sent out Light, and Firmament, and Earth, and Sea, and Sunne, and Moone, to give dignity to mans procession', Donne preached.

As the churches in England became increasingly plain and unadorned, the spectacular excesses of the court became presentations of the glories of heaven. Wrapped in religious rhetorics that blended a Puritan attention to scripture with a Catholic cult of image devotion and various occult elements culled from the Egyptian writings of Hermes Tristemegistus, a new politics of the state was emerging, a new mythology in which one's profession of faith was also one's profession of national identity.

The visible display of power was not simply the order of the day for monarchs. In Rome, too, there was an investment in making concrete the presence of God. It took the form of an exaggerated attention to surfaces: the barley-sugar twists and tasselled marble drapes of the ornate baldachin by Bernini in St Peter's; the gasps of ecstasy on the faces of his Theresa and the blessed Ludovico Albertoni. The Baroque announces an 'in your face' triumphalism, with its voluptuous forms, its expressive energies and its monumentality. The multifigured scenes (many of them scriptural or based on the lives of the saints) of Carracci and Rubens evidence a culture of enthusiasm for excess and extreme. On the borders of the Baroque lies the aesthetics of both the sublime and the kitsch. 'Baroque' was

45

a derogatory term for the extravagant and whimsical, grotesque, and even coarse and vulgar. On the other side of the *trompe-d'oeil* visions of eternity lies caricature, born at the same moment after Annibale Carracci. James I's self-conscious theatricality, his attention to what he termed a king's 'chiefest earthly glory', was being enacted elsewhere in Rome. In a passionate rhetoric of gestures and an erotic candour all brought to the depthless surface of the work itself, the Catholic church committed itself to a grandeur made visible. It is evident in the decoration of chapels and monuments, the number of votive pictures, paintings from scripture, baldachins, altarpieces, statues of saints, the designing of churches and the patronage of popes like Sextus V (1585–90) and Paul V (1604–21). As I said at the beginning of this chapter, the urge for the absolute conceived as material excess is not just a postmodern phenomenon. It has a Christian heritage.

The draw of the absolute towards the sublime, the ineffable, what Donne coined the 'superinfinite', and the pull of the material towards the pompous and the theatrical, both betokened and required a certain violence. Donne himself, an urgent and ambitious advocate of the king's glorious and divine dominion, preached both sides of a cosmic divide that the human body encompassed. While at times, in prose as in poetry, rehearsing the common Renaissance conceit of man as a microcosm of the macrocosm – 'the whole world hath nothing, to which something in man doth not answere' – Donne nevertheless marked the crisis of such a humanism:

> Is this the honour which Man hath by being a *litle world*, That he hath these *earthquakes* in him selfe, sodaine shakings; these *lightnings*, sodaine flashes; these *thunders*, sodaine noises; these *Eclypses*, sodaine offuscations, and darknings of his senses; these *blazing stars*, sodaine fiery exhalations; these *rivers of blood*, sodaine red waters? Is he a *world* to himselfe onely therefor, that he hath inough in himself, not only to destroy, and execute himselfe, but to presage that execution upon himselfe.

This is the first of his Meditations upon an illness he thought would kill him, published in a volume entitled *Devotions upon Emergent Occasions* in 1624. In fact, he had the book ready for the press

46

before he left his sickbed. His body is figured here as not only a landscape vulnerable to elements both mundane and celestial, but also as a body politic. 'Emergent Occasions' employs the language of statecraft. His body has become – in Donne's typical overreaching of both himself and his language – a nation in a state of emergency. 'The *disease* hath established a *Kingdom*, an *Empire* in mee, and will have certain *Arcana Imperii, secrets of State*, by which it will proceed' (Meditation 10).

While material excess fashions a new human aspiration for absolutist power, eyes were turning to the wider cosmos and a new concept of the infinite was born. This infinite relied upon a new mathematics to calculate the measureless. The body was being pulled apart, it was out of joint with the universal harmonies conceived by the imagination. It was subject both to internal and external violences. In fact, we have prefigured in Donne's prose the implosion of a world that saw itself as self-grounding and autonomous; he presages the self-destructive power of the secular. The body of the state, the body of the king, was racked and infected so that no rhetorics and shows of power, no myths of Sun Kings and Solomonic ceremonies, could contain what Donne describes as 'the ill affections of the *spleene.*'

In the afternoon of 14 May 1610, on the rue de la Ferronnerie, Paris, Henri IV, King of France, who had for years fought to work with both the Catholic League and the Protestant Huguenots, was stabbed three times in the chest by a Catholic and killed. In 1618 a 'general war that had been threatening ever since Henri's death'[3] erupted with all the brutality and sadistic passion evident in Donne's sermons and holy sonnets. And so began the Thirty Years War – the most distempered of the seventeenth century's so-called 'Wars of Religion'. In 1622 James was forced to issue his controversial *Directions for Preachers* in an attempt to suppress the growing religious dissension in the country.

Within the body and soul of John Donne the wars of religion had been waging for some time, at least since the death of his brother Harry in Newgate Prison in 1593. Like the prince, Donne saw himself as an *exemplum*, and it is as an *exemplum* that we can appreciate not only the distemper caused by those wars, but also something of the way they will be resolved. The conflict is laid out by

Donne possibly as early as 1593 (following his brother's death?), and certainly no later than 1597, in the third of his satires, 'On Religion':

> Seeke true religion. O where? Mirreus
> Thinking her unhous'd here, and fled from us,
> Seekes her at Rome; there, because hee doth know
> That shee was there a thousand yeares agoe,
> He loves her ragges so, as we here obey
> The statecloth where the Prince sate yesterday.
> Crantz to such brave Loves will not be inthrall'd,
> But loves her onely, who at Gevena is call'd
> Religion, plaine, simple, sullen, yong,
> Contemptuous, yet unhansome; As among
> Lecherous humors, there is one that judges
> No wenches wholsom, but coarse country drudges.
> Graius stayes still at home here, and because
> Some Preachers, vile ambitious bauds, and lawes
> Still new like fashions, bid him thinke that shee
> Which dwels with us, is onely perfect, hee
> Imbraceth her, whom his Godfathers will
> Tender to him, being tender, as Wards still
> Take such wives as their Guardians offer, or
> Pay valewes. Carelesse Phrygius doth abhorre
> All, because all cannot be good, as one
> Knowing women do in divers countries go
> In divers habits, yet are still one kinde,
> So doth, so is Religion.

The tone is witty and vicious; complex currents of contending emotions strive to find an articulate focus. It is not simply that Donne sets out four different candidates for the title of 'true religion', emphasizing their absolute claims to that title with the repetition of 'one' or 'onely'. The similitudes he develops with respect to each are suggestive and caustic. The veneration of the 'ragges' of the old religion is coupled with the veneration of civic reliques; the self-righteous austerities of the Calvinist tips over into a comparison with a perverse sexual appetite for 'rough trade'; affiliation to the Church of England comes about through the not-so-pious practices

48

of verbal seduction, legal injunctions and economic threats upon a fatherless child; the agnostic views religion simply as women's costume, different coverings for the same gender. If this last conceit holds less of a sting, even manifests a certain tolerance, the stance is nevertheless condemned by Donne as a form of indifference ('carelesse'), and the very bite in these lines betrays an inability to be indifferent while paralysed by the alternatives:

> but unmoved thou
> Of force must one, and forc'e but one allow . . .
> Be busie to seeke her, beleeve mee this,
> Hee's not of none, nor worst, that seekes the best.
> To adore, or scorn an image, or protest,
> May all be bad; doubt wisely; in strange way
> To stand inquiring right, is not to stray;
> To sleepe, or runne wrong, is. On a hugh hill,
> Cragged, and steep, Truth stands, and hee that will
> Reach her, about must, and about must goe.

The rebounding connotations of these words, the punning, the slipping and turning of the ideas, the juxtapositions, the violent contrasting movements of standing, straying and spiralling, betray not only Donne's enforced scepticism but the manner in which he theologically configures that scepticism in terms of a living purgatory. For the image of Truth on a huge hill is Dante's stage setting for the journey he makes between the inferno and paradise.

If to 'doubt wisely', rather than to be indifferent, is the first way ahead that Donne perceives (however tortuous), it was a way he turned from when in January 1615 (pushed by threatening penury as much as royal patronage) he became an Anglican minister. His sermons, until the death of James I in 1625, 'protest' loudly against Catholics and his Protestant credentials are stamped on every line: 'some grovell still in the superstitions they were fallen into and some are raised, by Gods good grace, out of them; and I am one'. He speaks then of 'one Religion', 'our Religion', 'the true worship of God' and 'the true religion' sometimes with such rhetorical force one wonders who he is attempting to persuade. But publicly at least (and the public nature of his testimony is an important factor here) he embraces the rigours of evangelical Protestantism (though not any of its sectarian variants) and the Puritan myth of the primitive church. And the 'true religion' having been sought is found.

Under Charles I Donne's sermons change in tone, scope and reference and something of a reconciliation takes place between his Catholic and Puritan pasts. Into his meditations on death and resurrection come suggestions altogether abhorrent to a Puritan: praying for the dead, 'the blood of Christ Jesus, *in* the Sacrament' (my emphasis), penance, the Inquisition, confessors. There are observations on reading Aquinas and the 'old Epistles of the Bishops of Rome'. Horror is registered at the ravishment of a cardinal, and his famous reference to sucking on the wounds of Christ resonates more with the poetry written later by the Catholic convert Richard Crashaw. A change seems to have taken place, or perhaps a new accommodation to a royal patron (Charles was recommending him for a bishopric by 1630 and when he died it was the High Churchman, Laud, who preached his funeral oration). But nothing is explicit.

'Seeke true religion. O where?' The question still vibrates for Donne, in public. But in private Donne is less guarded. In an unpublished sonnet, thought by scholars to have been written in 1620 and discovered by Sir Edmund Gosse in the late nineteenth century, we glimpse again something of the sceptic of the Third Satire, employing the same image of true religion standing on a hill.

> Show me deare Christ, thy spouse, so bright and cleare.
> What, is it she, which on the other shore
> Goes richly painted? or which rob'd and tore
> Laments and mournes in Germany and here?
> Sleeps she a thousand, then peepes up one yeare?
> Is she selfe truth and errs? now new, now outwore?
> Doth she, and did she, and shall shee evermore
> On one, on seaven, or on no hill appeare?

But the sonnet form (this is the octave) and the iambic pentameters bear none of the acerbic humour of the satire or the paradoxical tensions of thinking in two polarized directions. More significantly, the tonal contrast to sermons written in and around 1620 could not be more stark. Here the quiet, persistent, prayerful questioning that circles about the church as prostitute, as war victim, as millenarian hope; there the lambasting, importunate certainties of anti-Catholic invective. The Wars of Religion were about to receive their bloodiest catalyst on the Continent. Donne knew the different parties and all of Europe the dangers. Chaplain to the Earl of Doncaster, he was part of a diplomatic mission of mediation between the Catholic Holy Roman Emperor, Ferdinand, and the Palatinate of the Rhine, Frederick (married to James I's daughter Elizabeth in 1619). He had written a poem to celebrate the marriage of Frederick and Elizabeth, and he had stood in the presence of Ferdinand, recalling in one of his sermons that 'the greatest Prince (in style and title) . . . at the sound of a Bell kneeled downe in our presence and prayed; and God forbid he should be blamed for doing so'. This mission – always half-hearted, a royal gesture rather than an intervention – failed. By Christmas 1619 the mediators were home again. Frederick was roundly defeated at the Battle of White Mountain near Prague in 1620. The Catholic church celebrated by building Santa Maria della Vittoria in Rome, which housed Bernini's statue of St Theresa. But the defeat in Bohemia, as all Europe knew, left Frederick's lands in Germany exposed to the wrath of the Catholic League (with Descartes one of their enlisted number). The 'outcome of over half a century of religious confrontation between Catholicism and Calvinism'[4] was about to come to a head.

In private Donne ruminated, while publicly still he fulminated against 'the *Heretiques*' and 'the *Scismatiques* of our times' who 'multiple assassinats upon Princes and Massacres upon the people . . . as they mingle truthes and falshoods together in Religion'. And the private ruminations concerned reconciliation, not defences and distillations of the one and only 'true religion'. His last great sermon, published as 'Death's Duell' and thought to have been his own funeral address, alludes ambiguously to 'our God is the *God of all salvations.*' It is a small public expression that develops a line of thought found in a letter to his long-time friend Sir Henry Goodyear in April 1615 in which he wrote of 'that sound true opinion, that in all Christian professions there is a way to salvation'. Though, significantly, shying from entering into public debate – 'I will not, nor need you, compare religions' – he both confesses his conviction that 'God's mercies run through both [Puritan and Papist] fields; and

51

they are sister teats of grace' and his own sense that 'the Roman profession seems to exhale and refine our wills from earthly drugs and lees, more than the Reformed, and so seems to bring us nearer to heaven'. And yet he warns Goodyear not to go public on his opinions, for 'when you descend to satisfy all men in your own religion, or to excuse others to all, you prostitute yourself and your understanding, though not a prey, yet a mark, and a hope, and a subject, for every sophister in religion to work on'. The private man is divided from the public figure. It is the very necessity for such an enforced separation between the private and the public, between spiritual devotion and civic office, which points the way forward to an intellectual reconciliation of religions, on the one hand, and a political form of religious *détente*, on the other.

The Globalization and the Privatization of Religion

Donne could only dream of 'the Jesuits and the secular priests reconciled in England' subsequently 'press[ing] reconciliation to their Church'. But what theological basis for reconciliation was there? How does one proceed ecumenically before ecumenism? And what about those worshippers of other religions who stand etiolated at the edges of Donne's sermons and poetry – the Jews, the Turks, the American Indians, the believers in 'the transmigration of soules'? As threats, broken promises, political back-stabbing and finally war began to tear part the fragile and complex network of alliances in Europe a new discourse about religion was emerging, resourced by the Platonism of Ficino and the Italian humanists. It emerged from the diplomatic experience of one of Donne's closest acquaintances, Edward, Lord Herbert of Cherbury. Herbert may indeed have left on the same diplomatic mission as Donne in May 1619, only *his* specific brief was to become ambassador at the French court of Louis XIII. It is in the work of Herbert of Cherbury that the voice of what will become the modern philosophy of religion – the parent of the later sciences of religion – can first be heard.

Donne mentions nothing about the philosophical writings of Herbert of Cherbury, so we are unsure whether he read them. In

1619 many of their opinions would have been shared. For we find Herbert also writing back to James I, advocating support for his friend the Protestant Elector of Palatinate and castigating the machinations of the papacy and the Jesuits. His own job was to keep France neutral, an impossible task when James I, not revealing his hand to his ambassador, played with both the Spanish and the French. Donne was already back in England when war erupted and in August 1620 the French army went to the assistance of the Holy Roman Emperor and the Catholic League. Herbert, caught in a very difficult position, watched while the Protestant forces he supported were crushed, and continued the struggle to mediate between the parties. He left France, having failed in his mission, in August 1624. Cardinal Richelieu was just taking over as Louis's chief minister and the French involvement in the Thirty Years War was now about to be considerably stepped up – along with the persecution of Huguenots.

But before Herbert left France he published in Paris a remarkable book at the centre of which was that little word so vigorously being fought for all over Europe: truth. *De Veritate* transformed the thinking about what was true in 'true religion' by discarding both the Catholic appeal to the one true faith of the popes and the Protestant attempt to revive the primitive church as the one true religion. Herbert began with the philosophical question what is truth:

> Every truth can be analysed into truth of thing, truth of appearance, truth of concept and truth of intellect . . . All truth according to this doctrine consists of conformity. And since all conformity consists of a relation, it follows that all instants of truth will be relations, or aptitudes realized in act, that is in perception. No other way of describing truth is adequate.

Significant here is what counts as truth and, conversely, what does not. Later in life, when Herbert added remarks on religion and revelation, he also added a section on error. Truth lies in 'conformity' or correspondence between an object or event external to the faculties of the mind perceiving it and the faculties themselves. Truth lies in the harmony of the relation established whereby the mind is satisfied. This satisfaction is understanding.

53

What Herbert presupposed is twofold. First, that the mind operates according to a set of laws that can be investigated. Second, that there is an analogical relation between the world and the mind whereby we apprehend the nature of things by means of our innate faculties. We need not go any further into the complexities of Herbert's metaphysics; suffice it to say that Herbert stands between the Renaissance understanding of cosmological correspondences and what will be developed after John Locke as the correspondence theory of truth: that the truth of a proposition concerns the adequacy of the relationship between the object in the world under investigation and the concept of that object. What is important for us, with respect to the changing understanding of 'religion', is the move Herbert makes away from theological accounts of the soul towards a philosophical account of the psyche, the mind.

The Puritan worldview that sought for the primitive is the same worldview wanting to discover the foundational, that which is most certain, and those laws generating that certainty. The truth Herbert 'discovered' was both universal and self-evident. Self-evident, that is, to those who rightly use their reason. The self-evidence was not, yet, an appeal to self-validating empirical evidence; it remained the result of a certain idealism – but here was an attempt to 'begin upon the most certaine and unfallible Principles I could finde' (as he expressed in his autobiography, *Life*) which pre-dates Descartes's *Meditations on First Philosophy* by almost twenty years. In fact Descartes was reading a French translation of *De Veritate* in the years between writing *Discourse on Method* and the *Meditations*.

Herbert's text, with its emphasis upon 'just reason to believe', reveals the early dawning of modernity in the face of the Thirty Years War. The earlier clarion condemnations of 'superstition' and 'idolatry' had fostered a rationalization of religion; not just as practices of religious piety, but also in terms of articles or 'confessions' constituting the faith, and the institutions promulgating and policing such articles. Now the right use of reason as outlined by a new theory of knowledge and exercised by each individual in conformity with what is most natural and instinctive in all human beings, would define the nature and essence of religion itself. Religion would now not simply be an anthropological *a priori* (Ficino), but an epistemological *a priori* (that is, that which governs right reasoning and how

54

we arrive at knowledge of the world). A new relationship between faith and reason was under negotiation as a result of which truth would also become, as we will see, a moral principle applicable across all human cultures, histories and biographies.

In *De Veritate*, on the basis of his four categories of truth (of thing, appearance, concept and intellect) realized in the exercise of perception, Herbert deduced four overall operations of the mind: internal apprehension, external apprehension, discursive reasoning and natural instinct. Herbert called these 'faculties', but the word 'faculties' is overworked and is not always used unequivocally. These operations were hierarchically arranged so that the sense perception of things was related to concepts governed by the operations of the intellect. The first three faculties provided what Herbert termed 'Common Notions', but it was the final faculty, Natural Instinct, which was 'that mode of apprehension which springs from the faculties which conform to Common Notions'. With natural instinct Herbert located an internal apprehension of the truth, what Descartes would later term 'natural light'. Truth was known, then, instinctively; that is, in accordance with what in *Life* Herbert called 'Doctrines imprinted in the soul in its first original'. Through the operation of these innate and universal truths God's Grace and Providence worked within the world. True reasoning was but the application of these Common Notions or the working of this Natural Instinct that were stimulated when an object in the world was encountered. The Natural Instinct itself was higher than reasoning, enabling there to be perception of the transcendentals: the Good, the True, the Beautiful and the Just. Each transcendental was convertible to the others. The truths of the Natural Instinct were then what were most universal, most necessary and independent of all human feeling and thinking. The certainty they aspired to was mathematical – for 'all proof is derived from their principles'. They were stimulated by, but then evidenced, the conditions for making sense of practical experience.

In Herbert's rather unsystematic way of defining Natural Instinct and the Common Notions, religion (and the current religious dissensions) was at the forefront of his attention. Aware of the tensions between hardline Calvinists on predestination and followers of the Dutch divine Arminius, who placed an emphasis upon the freedom of the human will, he railed against a conception of God which would consign large parts of the human race to damnation. He railed also against the painted embellishments of the Catholic church. The concern to find a way beyond the details and particularities of these controversies is evident throughout.

> This [appeal to innate principles of universal truth and order] has never been so necessary as now. For men are now not only exhorted with every device that language can employ by arguments from the pulpit, but are tormented in spite of protests of conscience and the inner consciousness, by the belief that all who are outside their particular Church are condemned, whether through ignorance or error, to undergo instantly or with the concession of a short postponement, eternal punishment after death. The wretched terror-stricken mass have no refuge, unless some unmovable foundations of truth resting on universal consent are established, to which they can turn amid the doubts of theology or of philosophy.

And Herbert outlines the law of 'closest agreement concerning religion or civic and political justice'. The 'or' in that phrase is highly important. For what bound religion to civic or political justice – making them essentially the same – was virtue. It is the 'Common notions of God and virtue [which] occur everywhere'. Religion was fundamentally a moral practice. As he puts it in his *Life*:

> there be noe man that is given to Vice That doth not finde much Opposition both in his owne Conscience and in the Religion and Lawe as taught elsewhere, And This I dare say That a vertuous man may not onely goe securely through all the Religions but all the Lawes in the world and whatsoever obstructions he meete obtayne both an Inward peace and outyward wellcome among all with whom hee shall negotiate or Converse.

Ethics, like the price of gold, was the new common currency for universal harmony, and all else could be given over to the freedom of individual consciences or customer choice.

Later, Herbert expanded *De Veritate* and drew out in more detail the common axioms of all religions. He developed this thesis further in his long treatise *De Religione Gentilum*. What is both significant for the evolving nature of 'religion' and original, with respect to thinking about religions in the plural, is that Herbert treats not only different practices of Christianity, but also other world religions known at his time. His axioms, then, like the laws of science later (Newton's and Hooke's, for example), rely upon a process of inductive reasoning which had been championed by Francis Bacon. Having examined and compared the doctrines and forms of worship of Christianity, Judaism, Islam ('the Mohammedans'), the 'Egyptians and all the heathen races' (Greek and Roman), the 'East Indians', the 'Chinese' and 'the Indians of the West, Pachama Viracocha, etc.', then Herbert proposes what he describes in his *Life* as the five 'Poynts or Articles soe universally taught That they were not querstioned or doubted of in any other Religion I observed these five onely to bee Catholique and universal'. These are, as he lists them in *Life*:

1. That there is a supreme God. 2. That he is to be worshipped. 3. That vertue and Piety ioyned with Faith in and love of God are the best ways to serve and worship him. 4. That wee ought to Repent us of our Sinnes and seriously to return to God and the Right way. 5. That there is a reward and Punishment both in this life and after it.

Religion becomes 'the ultimate difference', the distinguishing characteristic of being human. Neither animals nor rocks are religious. No longer, then, do Columbus's Indians present some form of life prior to religion, for 'no period or nation is without religion'. Upon these five points rest all the authority of popes or presbyters, the priestly ornaments and the ceremonial embellishments that constitute the various religious practices. What Herbert believes he is distilling here is nothing less than 'the true Catholic or universal church'. And, putting aside whether these criteria can be said to cover all religions and irrespective of what influence Herbert may have had in the seventeenth century (and the scholars are divided here because of his convoluted Latin), the word 'religion' is not being used in the same sense in which Columbus, Shakespeare or Donne used it. Although he does not employ this language, religion can be understood now in terms of its essential form and its various outward expression. The outward expressions, he thought (and here his anti-Roman Catholicism is evident), were due to the priestly corruptions of the true religion. Herbert bequeathed this thinking to a series of prominent intellectuals who, in the seventeenth century and before the 'father of English Deism' labels were being composed, would further the project of the 'new' (the modern as opposed to the traditional) ways of knowing: Hugo Grotius (to whom Herbert sent a copy of *De Vertitate* before it was published), Mersenne (who may have translated *De Veritate*), Gassendi, Descartes and Locke.

It is important to understand the significance and implications of the move Herbert has made here. To arrive at his five-axiom archetype for the form of religion, ecclesiology, specific doctrinal content, liturgy and priestcraft have to been understood as secondary or epiphenomenal characteristics. At best these characteristics are in keeping with the five essential 'Notions', but Herbert was frank about 'imposture' and distortion. The true religion was without a church, without institutional ministrations, without teachings, disciplinings or the formation of followers through material practices. It was written in the hearts of humankind. Hence, although Christianity had been fundamental to defining the nature of this 'religion' (and the five Common Notions), the true religion has no role for Christ to play other than moral teacher and *exemplum*. The significance of the life of Christ (incarnation, crucifixion, resurrection), the doctrines of the triune God and the sacraments of grace were only secondary truths, to be understood metaphorically as particular expressions of the underlying universals. Herbert still finds room for revelation in his account of this natural religion. But the test of whether a revelation has taken place is whether what is said conforms to the innate universals. A cyclical logic is evident in which natural religion provides the conditions for understanding revealed religion and vice versa. The conditions for assessing the conformity include recognizing that 'the breath of the Divine Spirit [which] must be immediately felt'. In other words, final appeal is made to a spirituality, a pneumatology, whereby in inner sensations 'we feel the Divine guidance'. There are 'intimate divine apprehensions', a 'sense of succour', moments of 'intense faith' when we 'feel within us His saving power and a sense of marvellous deliverance'. Final appeal rests upon subjective judgement of inward emotional states made in accordance with the five universal laws constituting religion. A certain pietism lies waiting in this emphasis upon self-authenticating experience; a 'spirituality' is emerging that William James will catalogue in his famous Victorian tome *Varieties of Religious Experience*.

So although Herbert's hope is that civil strife and religious contestation will be resolved by the application of his 'sacred maxims', the means of the resolution is by withdrawing what is essentially religious from the public domain of institutional and personal practices. There is a deepening of the subjective turn towards personal salvation. The corollary of Herbert's ideas is that religious beliefs and affiliations become a private matter that can be judged only by one's own conscience. Publicly what is necessary is the outworking of or conformity to the moral code, the virtues of love, repentance and forgiveness. The dualism of this sentiment is affirmed metaphysically in the establishment of a division between the soul and the body. Herbert anticipates Descartes in suggesting that the body is merely a house for the mind. It is the mind and its Common Notions that will be punished or rewarded after death. The only way to keep the body politic in order is to distance or denigrate the physical bodies of those composing it. The metaphysical dualism, subsequently developed by Descartes and determinative for the way 'religion' is understood right up until postmodernity, can be seen as the offspring of a need to find a way beyond the dissensions, divisions and paradoxes of religious embodiment and its practices of piety. When John Locke in his famous *A Letter Concerning Toleration* (written in 1685 but not published in English until 1689) argues 'All the life and power of true religion consists in the inward and full persuasion of the mind', he is simply expounding the politics of this philosophical dualism. The private concern with salvation enjoins that the churches should have no 'jurisdiction in world matters', concerning themselves with the 'externals' of worship. While, on the other hand, civil government provides for the temporal good and the outward prosperity of society. The boundaries between the two are 'fixed and immoveable. He jumbles heaven and earth together, the things most remote and opposite, who mixes these two societies.' A profound secular space has now been conceived through the delineation of civil jurisdiction and power. The secular is now an independent, autonomous, neutral and objective space – something like the vacuum produced in the laboratories of Robert Boyle.

Herbert did not live to see the termination of the Thirty Years War with the Peace of Westphalia in 1648. The role religion had played in the war has always been a matter of some debate among historians. By 1648 it was more a matter of establishing rights to land; religion had been transmuted into moral geography. What the Peace established was a certain *détente* among Catholics and Protestants in Germany. Herbert did live to witness the outbreak of hostilities between royalists and parliamentarians in the English Civil War, and the continued toxic blend of politics and Christian enthusiasm that continued until the 1689 Act of Toleration. The Act itself granted Protestant dissenters (Presbyterians, Congregationalists, Baptists and Quakers) the right to worship freely alongside the state Church of England. Catholics and any religious practice that did not accept the trinitarian nature of God remained excluded; the Catholics because of the Jacobite threat following James II's flight from England to France. 'Religion' as it emerged in modernity was a Protestant Christianity, fostering a Protestant culture. It was monotheistic and Bible-based, and on these twin foundations a social consensus was possible that eventually even the Jewish people could adapt to. This social consensus and basis for religious pluralism remained in place until quite recently. But the tolerance it succeeded in establishing was a profoundly compromised and pragmatic one at best. It awaited the birth of an ideology that would underpin its moral and political foundations, naturalizing them: liberalism. Herbert's levelling of religions logically demanded absolute toleration, but this could only come about when a new understanding of human liberty – its value and the need to safeguard it – and a new understanding of being human, had emerged. Herbert had set out the axioms for a universal account of human nature – albeit a *homo religiosis* – but in a cultural context of political absolutism. There needed to come about a democratization of the idea of sovereignty, so that one person as an instance of the universal might represent several others, and the house of those representatives might enshrine a set of rights extended to all human beings.

Intellectually that new understanding of human rights and liberty was already taking shape in the late decades of the seventeenth century. The line of Stuart kings, with their divine rights, ended with the arrival on the shore at Torbay, on 5 November (the irony was fully understood), of William of Orange. Defoe, an enthusiastic supporter of William, saw this acceptance by the British government of the House of Hanover as a 'mutual contract'. Intellectually, a new understanding of governmentality and human nature was taking shape. In practice we have been struggling to realize its abstract ideals ever since. The preface to John Locke's *Letter Concerning Toleration* proclaimed 'Absolute liberty, just and true liberty, equal and impartial liberty, is the thing we stand in need of'. Whether these words are Locke's or his translator's, the *Letter* itself is much in line with Herbert's thinking – although Locke had challenged Herbert's notion of the innate ideas. True religion is instituted, he wrote, for 'the regulating of men's lives, according to the rules of virtue and piety'. True religion is instituted for the stability of the state. Like Herbert, Locke advocated the right use of reason with respect to religions. He composed a defence on *The Reasonableness of Christianity*. Like Herbert, Locke, in the 1690 additions to his *Essay on Human Understanding*, drew a distinction between types of revelation. And although he recognized the acceptance of certain religious propositions on the grounds of their being revealed truths, he argued strongly that reason had to judge 'the Truth of its being a Revelation'. '*I believe, because it is impossible*, might, in a good Man, pass for a sally of zeal; but it would prove a very ill rule for them to chuse their opinions, or Religions by.' But one notes in this sentence the word 'rule' and the verb 'chuse': there is a new sense of the freedom of the individual to decide and the need for that decision to be governed by the universal rules of right reason. Locke places great emphasis upon churches as 'free-voluntary' societies.

Religion has become now a matter of choice where freedom is defined as the ability to chose in accordance with one's own conscience. Freedom of conscience becomes the private corollary of the freedom from prejudice and the violation of one's life or property as civil rights maintained by public justice and equity. Religion now participates in a more general politics of politeness and taste. The stage was set for the liberalism of the modern secular state, the humanism that would forge the various declarations of human rights and the notion that human liberty must be maximized and infringements of it restricted to only those most necessary for social flourishing. But the liberalism, the humanism and even the notion of toleration are and will remain closely tied to a demystified Protestant Christianity. That demystification in terms of a true religion that was universal, exercised in and upon Christianity by Christians, would always bear the hallmarks of its specific legacy. As it increasingly shed its explicit Christian character it became less able to enquire into whose universals were being propounded, for whose benefit; and whose universals were being denied. In 1627, when Herbert's scholarly friend Hugo Grotius composed his own *De Religione Christianae*, he opens the first section of Book I with a reference to the Dutch fame as seamen. He writes what will become a systematic account of Christianity in which 'variety of opinions is limited within certain bands, in which all men are agreed' so that these seamen in their voyaging may confute errors. 'For they can never want matter, but in their long voyages will every where meet either with pagans, as in Chine or Guinea, or Mahometans, as in the Turkish or Persian Empires, and the the kingdoms of Fez and Morocco; and also the Jews.' While embracing some of Herbert's universals (he was one of the first readers of *De Veritate*) – there is one God and he is eternal, omnipotent, infinite, omniscient, good and the cause of all – Grotius nevertheless outlines the superiority of Christianity. It is the religion 'most agreeable to right reason' and so, armed with Grotius's statement of the agreed faith, seamen were informed as to how to confute the other religions – pagans (Book IV), Jews (Book V) and Mahometans (Book VI).

The modern understanding of rational 'religion', the 'true religion', has never been able to shake off its Protestant Christian roots. Later, in the late eighteenth and nineteenth centuries, a more developed 'evolutionary' account of religion made Christianity again the summit of a progression from polytheism to monotheism. And here at the end of the seventeenth century Locke exhorts ideas on tolerance and civil government in the name of Christian charity and the Prince of Peace and in an attempt to displace sectarian animosity onto a common cause: civic immoralities. With Locke there is a move beyond the displacement found in Grotius – the locating of a common Christian enemy abroad – because Locke maintained that toleration on the basis of civil government required that Jews and Muslims who consented to be members of the commonwealth should have the same right to freedom of conscience in the practices of their beliefs as Christians. But it is a displacement all the same from within the logics, emphases and recent histories of Christianity.

Liberalism would always remain a Protestant Christian project with imperial inspirations. In the transparency of the 'Christian' truth deducible by reason, now defining the moral nature and essential principles of religion, certain invisibilities were well and truly concealed, important invisibilities that, in becoming visible centuries later, would question the whole liberal edifice. This reasoned truth founded upon dualisms which exalted the mind above the body, is white, Western European, Christian in orientation, male (in so far as it constructs the female as other, as body, as sensual and irrational) and thinks in 'straight' (rather than queer) lines. As Herbert understood, the universal operation of reason called for depended upon an understanding of what constituted the 'normal' reasoner.

> Since the Common notion of a rose coincides in man's experience, all men will agree with me that objects which affect the whole of the faculties in the same manner produce the same results. I measure, therefore, the entire race by myself, and I assert (it is an instant of the Common Notion) that the same faculties have been imprinted on the soul of every normal person in all ages.

All 'men' might well agree, whatever might be understood by 'man' – for the modern understanding of the humanity of 'man' was also in cultural production at this time.[5] But this democracy of reason relies entirely upon a consensus concerning what it is that constitutes the 'normal' and the 'man'. It is no cultural coincidence that this appeal to the 'normal' arises at a time when the abnormal and the subnormal are being defined, when madness and the institutions for the housing and curing of the insane appear. What religion has become in postmodernity, as we shall see in chapter four, comes about through questions like 'whose rationality' is being articulated here? What is the 'norm' that defines the normal? What is man with respect to the processes of gendering and the exclusions operating with respect to those processes? What religion is, in postmodernity, is partly produced by the deconstruction of modernity's understandings of the moral nature and essence of religion; a deconstruction that comes about by rendering those invisibilities visible such that the questions can be asked whose rationality counts here, and for whom, and whose rationality is being discredited?

All this lies in the future. For the moment what is significant is the relationship between this abstract notion of natural religion, fundamentally an ethical account of religion, and colonial expansion. For the development of man as a religious animal brings with it the recognition that man is a cultural, political and commercial animal. Man is subject to an acquisitive desire. Locke in his *Letter Concerning Toleration* speaks out against 'the insatiable desire for dominion' which has used the gospel and the precepts of charity as masks for its rapaciousness. Locke composed the letter in Latin, and whether deliberately or by accident the words *dominandi libidine* echo St Augustine's understanding of the perverse desire that operates in sin: *libido dominandi*. The civil government Locke extols is the means for controlling the arrogation of power in the collapse and decline of ecclesial jurisdiction. With the public good as the rule that all citizens consent to, and the business of the churches understood to be the care and salvation of the soul, the bodies of human beings are given over to the disciplines, pleasures, securities and punishments of an accountable (and therefore seemingly transparent) domain called the commonwealth. Nevertheless, what emerges is a universalism paralleling the development of a market economy on the one hand, and privatization of beliefs, on the other; world trading (and the capitalist economies necessarily involved in and generated by such trading) and religion as the domain of subjective experience; civic duty (even civic religion or the state church) and matters of individual religious conviction. The politics of imperialism remained, even though operating now not in terms of the absolute sovereignty of the king, but through the flourishing of the middle-class merchants and tradesmen. 'No one seems to have seriously thought that William [III] was God's direct representative on earth.'[6] The relationship between monarch and people was a mutual, secular, contract.

In 1694, on the basis of a loan for £1,200,000 accepted by William III, the Bank of England was founded (and the national debt incurred). The road was open to the development of a credit culture. In the previous year Dr Richard Bentley published the first series of eight Boyle lectures (established in 1691) in which he traced the 'visible Footsteps of divine Wisdom' in the Frame of the world in a highly systematic *Confutation of Atheism*. The universal presence of God was revealed in creation by its exquisite organization and design. Surprisingly, having worked methodically through three main arguments in an *a posteriori* demonstration, Bentley concludes the lectures with an appeal to a divine pragmatics: 'For such a Usefulness of Things as neither proceeds from the Necessity of their Beings, nor can happen to them by Chance, doth necessarily infer, that there was an intelligent Being, which was the Author and Contriver of that Usefulness'. The order is not only organized and beautiful, it is efficient and useful. As Weber reminds us, the 'systematic utilization of goods and personal services' is the fundamental logic of capitalism.[7] Providence, free trade, the acquisition of material and temporal goods, and natural religion were creating a new set of social dynamics producing a cultural order in which natural science was convertible to moral science, which in turn was convertible to divine science. The rationalization of nature, being human, temporal goods, and government were related analogously to the rationalization of God. The God of this religion was not simply a divine Architect (Kant) or a divine Mathematician (Newton), HE (emphatically) was a divine Bookmaker – the one to whom one tendered one's accounts of one's own usefulness. As such, not only did 'natural philosophy constitute a religious practice',[8] so did good stewardship or use of creation's resources. The tradesman's calling is as good as any priest's (or scientist's), and for Dissenters like Daniel Defoe (who published his *Complete English Tradesman* in 1726), even better.

I Furnish Myself with Many Things: *Robinson Crusoe*

I was gotten home to my little tent, where I lay with all my wealth about me very secure. It blew very hard all that night, and in the morning, when I looked out, behold, no more ship was to be seen; I was a little surprised, but recovered myself with this satisfactory reflection, viz., that I had lost no time, nor abated no diligence to get everything out of her that could be useful to me, and that indeed there was but little left in her that I was able to bring away if I had had more time.

Daniel Defoe published *Robinson Crusoe* in 1719, after several years obsessed with accounting through a series of fights against bankruptcy. And several more years would follow. The novel is set in the mid-seventeenth century. In fact, Robinson's elder brother, we are told, died fighting in the Thirty Years War for the Protestants. Robinson, it seems, comes from Dissenter stock and a family of traders. With Defoe, Herbert's *homo religiosis* confronts the full implications of the *homo economicus*, and the disciplines of fate he receives fit him for becoming a *homo politicus* – a citizen in the City of Man, the Man of Reason. The interior pieties of conscience wrestle with the opportunities and pleasures afforded by the world; providence is pitted against the highly inventive and enterprising skills of the self-determined man; the remote and secret workings of the divine encounters the feverish speculations of the secular. What emerges is the very insecurity of the secular space that the new understanding of 'religion' worked within and brought about. The passage above illustrates in a nutshell the tensions exhibited throughout the novel. Here the certain fragility of existence (home as a tent), exposed to the winds of fortune that blow through the night, and the need for security, find consolation in the location of security in the accumulation of temporal goods ('all my wealth'). The possession of these goods, and the greed for them, is justified on the moral grounds of persistent, individual effort and utility. Labour is now a religious practice, a civic virtue. The ship (gendered female, like Nature, and crammed with goods that are there for the taking) is a metaphor for an opportune event. The centre of concern is the I, the me, the myself (mentioned ten times in the two sentences). Everything serves that I (gendered male) – except time ('if I had had more time') and the natural elements, both of which give opportunity as well as take it in a manner not simply beyond human control and foresight, but indifferent to it.

It is the insecurity of the new modern subject that gives rise to narration itself. The early novel, the picaresque novel, is founded upon insecurity. Years pass on the island without comment because 'reduced to my [former] calm, sedate way of living'. These are not narratable years. Change, chance, fortune, providence, fate and opportunity are the stuff of novels, dramatized in *Robinson Crusoe*, as in the peregrination novel more generally, by movement. The tensions then between self-determination and the guiding hand of God, between the secular and the religious, between nationalism and globalism, between humane and inhumane conduct, between different religions, between nature and manufacture, are all staged in terms of dramatic confrontations throughout the novel between Crusoe and the Moors, or the Negros, or the savage creatures, or the cannibals, or the sea, or the climate, or the absence of the right kinds of equipment.

The writing of accounts – the lists Crusoe continually makes of his resources, the charts he draws up of the annual weather system, the numbering of the cannibals he kills, the journal he keeps in his first year, and the book itself as an account of a 'private man's adventures' – is an attempt to remain in control, to understand how the finest of details is part of the whole design. The 'private' self does not mediate but rather rides the tensions in order to demonstrate and be exercised in virtuous self-government. The mastery of one's surroundings – Crusoe will see himself as absolute ruler of the island – and one's adversities ('I seldom gave anything over without accomplishing it') were required and needed to express a fundamental self-mastery, an internalized disciplining.

> I was absolute Lord and lawgiver; they all owed their lives to me, and were ready to lay down their lives, if there had been occasion for it, for me. It was remarkable, too, we had but three subjects, and they were of three different religions. My man Friday was a Protestant, his father was a pagan and a cannibal, and the Spaniard was a Papist. However, I allowed liberty of conscience throughout my dominions.

We can view the whole story of *Robinson Crusoe* as an imaginative experiment in moral and political education, an *éducation sentimental*.

67

Through the redemption of a young, enterprising but godless man from his wicked ways, a nation is being instructed in the path to citizenship. The novel is composed of a thought-experiment – as inductive in its way as the experimentation going on under the watchful eyes of the Royal Society – in which a human being can be placed within a limited set of conditions and observations made upon his responses. The observations frequently give way to laws of human behaviour or moral principles:

> this just observation . . . viz., how frequently, in the course of our lives, the evil which in itself we seek most to shun, and which, when we have fallen into, is the most dreadful to us, is oftentimes the very means or door of our deliverance, by which alone we can be raised again from the affliction we are fallen into.

We can note here how these 'observations' employ a Christian language of fall and deliverance, the onset of evil and being 'raised again'. The discourse shifts between a specific Christian practice and universal sentiments of a proto-psychological and moral nature. Christian ethics is becoming public morality, public truth. This is characteristic of what happens to 'religion' in *Robinson Crusoe*. So the 'wickedness of my past life', when examined, turns out to be as much anti-social ways of living as vices of a Christian soul: his disobedience and finally desertion of his parents; his inability to settle down and establish himself. Furthermore, Crusoe's own education of the cannibals and re-education of the mutinous crew are exercises in the ways of Western civility – a natural propensity to which is read as a mark of God's providential design. As Friday tells Crusoe, 'You teach wild mans be good sober tame mans'. For this reason, when Jean-Jacques Rousseau in 1762 conducted his own imaginative exercise in moral education, in *Émile*, he considered there 'is one book which, to my thinking, supplies the best treatise on education according to nature. This is the first book Émile will read . . . it is *Robinson Crusoe*.' The moral centre of Crusoe's redemption is his becoming humane: 'Principles of tenderness, or the common bowels of pity to the miserable . . . is reckoned to be a mark of generous temper in the mind', he writes, having castigated the Spanish for their 'barbarities practiced in America . . . unjustifiable

68

either to God or man'. Once humane there is 'deliverance'. And, as Crusoe returns to international trading, the deliverance takes the form of a freedom to engage in commercial society.

Crusoe's moral-education-as-salvation-to-trade begins with his shipwreck on the desert island, which dramatizes St Paul's observation to Timothy that 'By rejecting conscience, certain persons have made shipwreck of their faith'. Conscience mediates between Christian piety and public morality. Prior to the shipwreck Crusoe's scrabbles for his own preservation and flourishing have been at the expense of other people: Xury, his young Muslim companion and the Africans he is ready to ship to Brazil as slaves for the other plantation owners. So, on the island, he first has to discover the secret murmurings and promptings of his conscience. Nature prepares him for what revelation will complete, for the turning point of this section of the story is Crusoe's dream, while ill, of God descending and threatening to kill him because the good orderings of his providence have not brought him to repentance. With repentance comes insight: 'I had rejected the voice of Providence'. It is the voice of providence that enables Crusoe to read the world aright. Bentley's 'visible Footsteps of the divine Wisdom' can be read in the book of nature, if this book is read through the word of scripture as it resonates in the tenderized conscience. This lesson is learnt while mastering his surroundings and therefore, in his preservation, his own destiny. Its perfection is reached in those moments of satisfaction, when Crusoe, having become the ideal, Adamic husbandman governing his Eden and using its resources well, blesses God for its goodness.

The discovery of the famous footprint initiates a second phase in that education, for it unsettles again the self-mastery and control acquired. The thought of a 'nation' of cannibals visiting the island, even if only occasionally, invokes a profound disturbance. Crusoe, who has been so concerned with self-cultivation, encounters the other – the savage, the bestial, the uncivilized, that which not only disregards what it is to be human, but confounds the very understanding of what it is to be human (by consuming each other). The newly emerging doctrine of Man was haunted by this figure of the cannibal, as we will see again in the next chapter. Cannibalism is the destructive hysterical note in the narcissism of cultivating autonomous individuals. 'These anxieties, these constant dangers I lived in, and the concern that was now upon me, put an end to all invention and to all the contrivances that I had laid for my future accommodations and conveniences.' The encounter with Friday shows how unnecessary his fears and anxieties were: 'he had all the sweetness and softness of an European in his countenance'. For Friday is a poor man in need and so no threat to Crusoe the superior white Prince of his dominions.

With Friday Crusoe repeats, with respect to another person, the education he had himself received: an education in morals, government and civility. The pupil becomes the teacher. But unlike the Indians in the journals of Christopher Columbus, Friday's 'nation' (as Crusoe continually calls it) are not 'without religion'. And, from the point of view of the transformation of the understanding of 'religion' with respect to Christianity, the education Crusoe gives is significant for the tensions it raises and cannot resolve. These tensions are at the heart of emerging liberal governmentality itself, of liberal humanism itself. For Crusoe, in now becoming a self-appointed hand of providence, sets about 'instruct[ing] him in the knowledge of the true God'. Friday's god, old Benamuckee, gives way to he who 'governs the world by the same Power and Providence by which He made it'. Yet at a striking moment Crusoe and Friday discuss the omnipotence of this God, the role of Jesus Christ and the presence of the Devil. And Crusoe finds himself unable to instruct Friday as to why God, in his omnipotence, did not put an end to the Devil, and short-circuit the road to redemption. The necessity of Jesus Christ in this rational account of divine salvation, his 'usefulness' (to use Bentley's term), is left undemonstrated. This needs to be revealed to Friday, Crusoe concludes, and prays that it will. But we are never shown whether it is. And although we are told that Friday is a 'Protestant', the role of Jesus Christ is attenuated in Defoe's Christian theology. It is this very attenuation that allows the 'liberty of conscience' which predominates throughout the novel; just as this attenuation allows for consensus and toleration in the monotheistic and biblicalist culture of liberalism. For there is no comment on the religion of the Turks in the early part of the novel and there are considered apologia for withholding judgement of the pagan cannibals on several occasions. This liberty of conscience nevertheless vies with a missionizing zeal to convert the heathen by impressing upon them white, European supremacy, and white, European rationalism. Furthermore, the liberty of conscience is granted by the 'absolute lord and lawgiver'. 'He has bestowed upon them the same powers, the same reason, the same affections, the same sentiments of kindness and obligation, the same passions and resentments of wrongs, the same sense of gratitude, sincerity, fidelity, and all the capacities of doing good and receiving good that He has given to us', Crusoe says on encountering Friday. But in this promotion of the universal rights of man, some human beings are nevertheless more equal (and universal) than others.

What has been called the 'advancement of the colonial/imperial vision' offered by Defoe's book[9] is inseparable from a Christianization in which the role of Jesus Christ is increasingly less 'useful'. What remains 'useful' are the virtues enjoined by Christianity – tenderness, compassion, generosity, hospitality, courage, temperance, hope, gratitude, benevolence, etc. – in the development of civil government. As Crusoe reflects, 'niceties in doctrines, and schemes of church government . . . were all perfectly useless to us'. Guided by the Spirit of God, there was no need for church or liturgy, only a Bible and a sufficiently responsive conscience able to discern the invisible hand. But unlike the paranoias of John Bunyan in *Grace Abounding to the Chief of Sinners* (1666), the convolutions of that discernment are not problematic for Defoe. They are not problematic because Crusoe has an adequate theory of interpretation that avoids the dangers of literalism, on the one hand, and metaphoricity, on the other. It is not problematic because most of the time Crusoe is so busy doing and making, planning and building, inventing and speculating, that the providence of God is simply allowed to remain invisible. As Defoe wrote in his 1701 essay *The Danger of the Protestant Religion*, 'the great Chain of Causes and Effects' is not frequently 'interrupted by God himself'. So there is a politics involved in making manifest the hand of God. It is only rendered visible when it is necessary, or even 'useful', to calm the fears and insecurities that continually arise in the secular space opened up by the remoteness of the divine and the free reign given to *homo economicus* to extend his dominion and 'furnish myself with many things'. A war continues to be waged, only this time between such abstractions as reason, conscience, passion, desire, public truth and public morality.

71

And all the appeals to liberal humanism will not assuage the tumultu-
ous soul conceived in the insecurities of modernity between the
invisibility of God and the invisibility of the true church.

Crusoe's deliverance is being set free for further speculations on
the erratic tides of international trade. The tale does not end on his
settlement back home; rather, he submits to his 'inclination' to
travel as a 'private trader'. No consultations are made with God on
this matter. God is quietly dropped in favour of a surrender to what
Defoe calls Providence but might just as easily be called Fortune,
and 'new adventures'.

'Defoe wrote *Robinson Crusoe* with a particular colonial project in
mind – British colonization in Spanish America – which is why he
located the island near the mouth of the Orinoco River', one
commentator notes. Certainly, the book on average went through
two editions each year throughout the Victorian period, when it
received its most attention and the imperialist vision flourished. Its
theme was rehearsed by Marrayat, Ballantyne and Stevenson. What
is significant is that from the early 1800s the book was often published in abridged forms, particularly for children, and in the abridged
forms the meditations of providence and the invisible God disappear
entirely.[10] The logic of that disappearance issues from the novel itself
and the worldview it represents. As the secular space swells and the
invisible God withdraws ever deeper into his own inner designs, so
atheism issues from the pursuit of the 'true religion'. But the world
is suddenly darker, and the threat of those who prey on human flesh
and blood will increasingly haunt the imagination of the West.

3

True Religion and Consumption

So much depended upon what Lord Herbert of Cherbury (without recognizing its political connotations) called 'conformity', and what later became known in philosophy of religion as the analogy from design. As William Paley, the eighteenth-century divine, argued in his influential book *Natural Theology, or Evidences of the Existence and Attributes of the Deity, Collected from the Appearances of Nature*, the discovery of a watch on an otherwise deserted beach would indicate the existence of a watchmaker. By analogy, then, the discovery of design in the world argues for the existence of a designer. The natural order maintained the moral order and the moral order maintained the political order *only* if it was assumed that there was an elaborate interconnectivity between the three to begin with. Only with the transcendent deity guaranteeing the rational order of things could the inductive reasoning that now lay at the foundation of natural, moral and divine science guarantee that the move from particular to general, empirical observation to apodictic law, demonstrated or proved anything of a theological nature. But what if there was no order? What if inductive reasoning could be seen as circular (only discovering in the particular the law already assumed to be there)? What if the natural order or the perception of order could be explained without the need for God? What if order was an immanent process or order was a construction of the mind upon what was otherwise chaotic and random sensations? Then 'religion' would begin to shift its meaning once again and enter another cultural context. Ethics would have to separate itself from religion and nature from both; the sinews of their intimate relationship – or Herbert's 'conformity' – would begin to tear. In the tearing the unsettling and dark infinity of what is other and unknown makes its appearance. Presciently, Pascal, in 1658, writes in his *Pensées*: '[I feel] engulfed in the infinite immensity of spaces whereof I know nothing, and which know nothing of me, I am terrified. The eternal silence of these infinite spaces alarms me.'[1] Here, being consumed by darkness was unsettling and presaged an intimation of a *deus absconditus*; for others, later, the darkness was to be welcomed as the ultimate consummation of truth.

Eclipse

... he sinks trembling with sweet anguish into the dark, alluring womb of nature, his poor personality being consumed in the breaking waves of delight, and nothing remaining but a focal point in the immeasurable procreative power, a sucking whirlpool in the vast ocean.

Thus wrote the poet, novelist, philosopher and theologian Friedrich von Hardenberg, who wrote under the pseudonym Novalis, in his early work *The Apprentices of Sais*. The fierce rationality of the Enlightenment suffered an eclipse in the late decades of the eighteenth century. Novalis, himself born during a total eclipse, captured the emerging *Zeitgeist* in his poems, aphorisms and fragments. *Hymns to the Night* was composed in the winter of 1799–1800. In the fifth and sixth sections of the poem, he articulates the very antipathy of salvation through the light of reason:

> One night of ecstasy –
> one durable poem –
> and our sun in space
> mirrors God's own face.

God is conceived within a new dazzling darkness. The yearning for a relationship with him demands an entry into night. Death is now erotically charged, aestheticized and at the heart of religion.

The world for Novalis is full of 'raging pain', the religious visions of the past are 'desperately lost' and

> With anxious longing our eyes search
> through the night's blue-black void.

Beckoned by those who have gone before, the poet draws towards the 'gulf' and ends the hymn with:

> Now we'll meet the star-bride,
> Jesus, and his company.
> Comfort in this grey twilight
> for those broken by their grief.
> A dream will lose us to the tide,
> and sink us in the father's womb.

The road to salvation lies through entering the deep and secret darknesses of night: 'life moves / into infinity'.

What is new here is a longing, nurtured in the poetry of the infinite, for a consummation and a comforting that will immerse the self and dissolve the boundaries of here and there, of dream and reality, of male and female, of birth and death, of day and night, of we and them. The longing is to be consumed – for the subject to be ultimately and finally negated by becoming one with the Absolute. The longing goes beyond the rational performance of one's moral duty, and beyond the economic business of subjugating, colonizing, exploiting and stewarding the goods of this world. A God is sought who is neither a watchmaker, nor an architect, neither a mathematician nor a bookmaker. God is no longer an omnipotent, omniscient, absolutely perfect person, nor an Archimedean point outside the system. God is all things and more. There is the same search for a world religion envisaged as universalized or essentialized Christianity, the search for the true religion, but having now circumnavigated the world the search is conducted extraterrestrially. The divine defines itself beyond abstract rational axioms in a new appeal to the intuition of infinity itself. Galaxies, constellations and the primordial chaos from which the cosmos issued offer a language more fitting to this new haunting by the infinite. An infinite Christianity is conceived which, while intimating an inexpressible unity, neverthe-less negates all present, terrestrial interests. The true religion con-sumes the world in order to transfigure it. 'Christianity will thereby become . . . the projecting force of a new world-structure and mankind . . . absolute abstraction – annihilation of the present – apotheosis of the future', Novalis wrote in a letter to Friedrich Schlegel. The universalism of the true religion works now with 'absolute negativity' and the poets sing of night and death and destruction: 'Genuine anarchy is the creative element of religion', Novalis wrote in his allegory of world history 'Christendom or Europe'. In *Hymns to the Night* personal names like 'Jesus' or 'Mary' hover on the near edge of an overwhelming oblivion. They are finite and particular moments on the point of disappearing into the ideal, spiritual universe discovered in Night. Night is 'the mighty womb of revelations'. Here is a diremption, an emptying out of the meaning and significance of the contingent and the concrete. There is, to use a technical theological term that became common at this time, a kenosis at the heart of the religious that is the operation of the universal itself.[2]

The 'we' of Novalis's poem refers to his fiancé, Sophie von Kuhn, who had died over two years earlier. Two months after her death, while visiting her grave (as he frequently did), he had a forceful experience of her presence with him. As he records it in the third hymn in a broken prose:

> The mound became a cloud of dust – through the cloud I saw
> the transfigured features of the beloved. Eternity rested in her
> eyes . . . Millennia moved off into the distance like storms.

The girl, who was only 15 years old when she died, has dissolved here into a nameless 'beloved', dissolving further into 'eternity' and then 'millennia'. This dissolution is conceived religiously, as a trans-figuration and, finally, the beloved is caught up into the embrace of Jesus the 'star-bride'. The girl, like Dante's Beatrice and Petrarch's Laura, figures a religious longing in the poet, a transcendental desire for things eternal, unutterable, sublime. In fact, by the time Novalis wrote *Hymns to the Night*, he was engaged to another woman, Julie von Charpentier. Woman as an abstraction figures and genders the religious, which is no longer rational but erotic. But it is a 'queered' woman, for the Night is a divine, paternal womb and, elsewhere, this woman is 'the veiled virgin' (Mary as the goddess Isis). Nevertheless, an eros drives the subject beyond the material and physical towards an unconditional point where words are silenced in a negation that offers, with a Romantic irony, infinite plenitude. As Novalis wrote in the first of the *Hymns*: 'Consume me with spirit fire that I may mingle ethereally and more intimately with thee, and the bridal night may last then forever'. This consumption, linked, as in Latin, to consummation, will reoccur in various forms throughout this new search for the true religion.

Novalis had been brought up in the Pietist tradition where spiritual mediation and emotional experience were encouraged. In fact, later Novalis made an unusual connection (for the time) between Pietism and the spiritual exercises of the Jesuits. But the religious experience in *Hymns to the Night* betrays the paradoxical tension between what Blake terms a 'dark secret' passion and a bloodless abstraction; the erotic is negotiated through allegory.[3] What emerges as religion is not a return to medieval orthodoxy, nor Protestant dogmatics, nor moral reasoning, but it is nevertheless a continuation – albeit with renewed energy – of the Christian religion's universalization. Religion from now on will define itself with respect to an experience of the unconditional; an experience recreated and performed through a new turn to allegorization that renders the materiality of the world resonant with what Novalis called a 'magic idealism'. The allegorization – understood both as an event transforming subjective perception of the world and as a literary form, a view of the world and a way of writing – accommodated a new religious syncretism. Novalis spun worlds in which Christian ideas of deification and sacramentalism culled from the early Greek Fathers found an elective affinity (Goethe's term) with Greek mythology, elements of Neoplatonism and the Eastern mystery cults of Isis. The allegorization allowed for a universalism that was neither a reduction to moral axioms nor an account of the condition of being human. It suggested a new way of conceiving religious plurality. A narrative (in fact a metanarrative) was being composed in which history was now History – as a movement into the future towards the realization of the fundamental unity of all cultural expression.

Creation had fallen (the Christian mythology remained strong) into fragments and atoms, but History would gather into the whole all the scattered parts. 'Only the whole is real', Novalis wrote.

Novalis found a friend who he believed to be of similar disposition. Certainly they shared a similar Pietistic background. Friedrich Schleiermacher, in the same year Novalis composed his hymns, had written what has become one of the most influential pieces of writing on the nature of modern 'religion': *On Religion: Speeches to Its Cultured Despisers.* 'Religion was the maternal womb in whose holy darkness my young life was nourished and prepared for the world still closed to it', Schleiermacher wrote in the first of his lectures. The image is almost an echo of Novalis's 'holy, ineffable mysterious Night'. It is no wonder Novalis read *On Religion* with rapture, penning his own 'Christianity or Europe' as a response. Though they never met, the two men 'corresponded' verbally through a mutual friend, Friedrich Schlegel. Novalis had met Schlegel while studying at the University of Leipzig. Schlegel encouraged and published Novalis's work as he did Schleiermacher's. In fact Schlegel lived with Schleiermacher for a time in Berlin, and when Novalis died in March 1801, at the age of 28, Schlegel was with him.

It was Schlegel, his brother Augustus, Alexander von Dohna (a young aristocrat who Schleiermacher had once tutored) and Henriette Herz (to whose fashionable Berlin salon Schleiermacher had been introduced) who constituted *On Religion*'s 'cultured despisers'. They were the audience for whom Schleiermacher composed his lectures – at their behest. What they were despising was twofold: the cold rational reduction of religion to morality, on the one hand, and a repressive Protestant theology which had been part of public policy under the Prussian King Friedrich Wilhelm II, on the other.

For Berliners, the Jewish philosopher Moses Mendelssohn epitomized the rationalization of religion. Significantly, in his prize-winning essay of 1763 ('On Evidence in Metaphysical Sciences'), he pinpointed how such rationalism had led to the rise of a class of sceptics: 'With the emergence of philosophy and the knowledge of nature, one also saw the emergence of atheists and those who scoff at religion, individuals who, by their discoveries, exposed the weak foundations of superstition and fancied they had overthrown all possible ground for the existence of God and his properties'. Here lay the intellectual roots of the rejection of religion by the 'cultured'. The backlash against both excessive rationalism and scepticism was a new call to Protestant orthodoxy. Books like Kant's *Religion within the Limits of Reason Alone* had been subject to public condemnation and Kant himself was forbidden to write anything more on religion, under this old regime.

By 1799 the edict concerning the constitution of religion in the Prussian state had been rescinded by the new king, Friedrich Wilhelm III. Schleiermacher had been in Berlin for three years, as the Reformed Chaplain to a hospital, during which time he had moved in the circles of what was an emerging German Romanticism. Herz's salon was literary and philosophical, but in conversations religious questions were still raised, while laughed at, for the Herz's were Jewish and strong defenders of Jewish emancipation. Friedrich Schlegel was courting Dorothea Viet, the married daughter of Moses Mendelssohn. Berlin, since Mendelssohn first established himself there, was the centre for the promulgation of a new image of Jewish citizenship.[4]

The Jewish question was an important aspect of the new developments in the term 'religion' and Schleiermacher's early involvement in redefining the nature or, now, the essence of such religion. The call for their full rights to citizenship was inseparable from secularization and the rise of the morally self-sufficient civic society. We noted in chapter 2 how Locke had seen religious toleration and civic integration as a consequence of liberal government. Later, in 1714, John Toland advocated the same case in his pamphlet 'Reasons for Naturalizing the Jews'. But Toland added a further, more pragmatic argument that returns us to the relationship between the universalization of religion and economic development: by naturalizing the alien one increased both the population and the wealth of a country. Natural religion therefore provided the philosophical basis for the politics of toleration, just as the rise of the nation-state provided the political basis for citizenship, and the wealth and fertility of the population provided the economic basis for what we now call sustainable growth. Earlier, the Christian rationale for the tolerance of the Jewish people had been evangelistic: they were a remnant of a dead form of faith that needed to be converted into the living, Christian faith. But increasingly this belief gave way to a complex weave of metaphysics, liberal humanism, economics and what Michel Foucault would call 'biopower'. Metaphysically, the Enlightenment fostered the notion of a common humanity in which religious allegiance was secondary to human rights. Politically, the nation-state fostered the demand for patriotic duty above religious observance. Economically, it was recognized that the Jews were a source of direct and indirect wealth for the secular state: as payers of the *Schutzgeld* (literally, protection money) — a tax levied on the Jews which allowed their toleration in a certain location — and as bankers and merchants with business connections extending throughout Europe. By the edict of 1812 Prussian Jews were granted the right of citizenship, but it was only in the wake of a necessary reorganization of the Prussian state following its defeat by Napoleon at Jena in 1806.

The emancipation and integration of the Jews was the litmus test for the universalization of religion, for they were the explicitly religious 'other' in the very courts, conurbations, provinces and municipalities of the Christian West. In Schleiermacher's *On Religion*, despite references to the multiplicity of religious forms, the only other specific religious practice referred to is Judaism. What is interesting is how the Jewish people themselves began to accept the generic word 'religion', how a process of acculturation occurred. A word formed by and through the universalization of Christianity, bearing still the watermarks of its tradition-based origin, began to be used as a term by practitioners of other pieties, of other faiths, to describe themselves. And this process of acculturation began with the Jews and their expression of the right to full citizenship in the countries in which they were born.

Moses Mendelssohn, son of a Torah scribe, a *Yeshiva* educated in the Bible and the Talmud, paved the way:

Heathens had the misfortune that their religion rested on such weak supports. Their priests wanted to ascribe each extraordinary natural event to the immediate working of some higher power. To hold a raw and uncultivated people in check, nothing is easier and more convenient than a system of religion

80

that completely surrounds us with divinities and teaches us to recognize the immediate working of a higher power in the rustling of every waterfall, in the voice of thunder or the stormy wind, in everything that stirs the senses.

'Religions' are systems that are more or less rational depending upon whether they are more or less cultivated, where 'cultivated' means the eradication of superstition and priestcraft. Mendelssohn accepted revelation and supported rational proofs for the 'existence of God and his properties'. But he also fused the metaphysics of deism with Protestant biblicalism and the monotheism of the Jewish faith in a way that placed him among the leading Enlightenment intellectuals of his day. With acculturation, the universalizing of religion was now not just legitimating an explicit colonial expansion; it was being internalized by those wishing to be colonized. For the state in which citizenship was being sought remained related to Christian patterns of social behaviour: Sunday observances, annual holidays, Protestant education, and the absence of dietary laws. Furthermore, as the pressure on Mendelssohn to make public statements about his beliefs demonstrates, the very acceptance of Enlightenment principles was 'interpreted as a halfway station on the way to Christianity'.[5] Henrietta Herz converted to Christianity following the death of her husband, and Mendelssohn's daughter, Dorothea, who eventually married Friedrich Schlegel, also turned to Christianity, finally publicly converting to Roman Catholicism.

Religion: Negative and Positive

The dissemination of 'religion' was taking new forms and, likewise, the definition of what religion consisted of – religion's essence. Mendelssohn, in his descriptions of conscience (the beating heart of religion-as-morality), again pointed the way. For he speaks of the conscience as 'The inner feeling, this sentiment of good and evil', and of a dynamic knowledge that effects desire and practice. But it is Schleiermacher who gives this passionate and affective understanding of religion its famous focus. In *On Religion*, religion's 'essence is neither thought nor action, but intuition and feeling'. By rejecting

81

'thought and action' as providing the grounds and content for understanding the divine, Schleiermacher is stepping beyond the rationalism [thought] and moralism [action] of Enlightenment religion. True religion was being conceived now as that which is the experiential condition for the possibility of both speculative thought and community action, the perception of the infinite in the finite. The essence of true religion lay in feeling and intuition.

It is important here to understand how the concept of 'intuition' is entwined in a complex philosophical history bequeathed to Schleiermacher, as to the other early Romantics like Novalis and Schlegel, from Kant. This very translation of a concept, related as it is in Kant to the mental faculty of the imagination, points to a cultural transformation *within* the Enlightenment tradition. Kant understands intuitions as the most basic apprehension of the 'sensuous manifold' or things as they are in themselves. Intuition is prior to thought, for thought requires concepts and concepts emerge spontaneously when intuition passes through the twelve categories of the understanding. The faculty of the understanding, and the faculty of reasoning which processes the thoughts that arise within the understanding, receive intimations of the world beyond consciousness through the faculty of the imagination. Intuition introduces the manifold sensations of what is into the imagination; it relates world to mind. The imagination synthesizes these 'blind' intuitions – 'blind' because until they are given conceptual form they cannot be thought as such. Nevertheless, Kant describes intuitions as both 'intellectual' in the sense that they are mental processes, resonances on the edges of consciousness, and 'sensible' in so far as they are related to sense perception. While they mediate the world to consciousness they also maintain a distinction between what Kant called the realms of the phenomenal (the world as it is constituted in and through the transcendental operations of the mind) and the noumenal (the *Ding an sich* or things as they are in themselves). The ontological is separated from the epistemological; what is from what I know of what is. As Andrew Bowie points out, for Kant, 'nature is threatened with disintegration into endless difference'.[6] In his later *Critique of Judgement* Kant explicitly related the intellectual nature of intuitions with feelings; the experiences of objects of pleasure and pain. The intuition is receptive and feeling spontaneously arises on this reception. Even so, the feelings cannot be directly related to the object since they arise in the cognizing subject. We cannot therefore know that it is the object as such which is giving the pleasure or the pain, only the effect of the object upon subjective consciousness. Kant could deduce a connection between the experience of the object and the experience of the cognition of the object, but he could not demonstrate a necessary relation. Feeling and intuition could not then, for Kant, be synonymous. They will become synonymous as the nineteenth century develops and religion becomes even more closely tied to mystical experience and feeling is understood as 'the deepest source of religion'.[7] It is significant for the early Romantics that in investigating the possibility for a relationship between intuition and feeling, Kant develops an account of the faculty of the imagination no longer entirely governed by the faculty of the understanding. The imagination has a freedom and power of its own. The dynamic and synthetic power of the imagination will become an influential idea.

Schleiermacher's association of feeling and intuition modifies Kant's view in favour of an immediate apprehension of a primary unity between mind and world. In the second lecture on the essence of religion, he emphasizes a 'feeling for the infinite' in which 'religion is the sensibility'. The 'universe's immediate influences' work powerfully upon the passive recipient, and Schleiermacher's argument hinges on the immediate relation between that universe and the perceiving subject:

> All intuition proceeds from an influence of the intuited on the one who intuits, from an original and independent action of the former, which is then grasped, apprehended and conceived by the matter according to one's own nature. If the emanation of light . . . did not affect your sense . . . if the pressure of weight did not reveal to you an opposition and a limit to your power, you would intuit nothing and perceive nothing, and what you thus intuit and perceive is not the nature of things, but their action upon you.

Both the proximity to and the modification of Kant are evident here. The threefold grasping, apprehending and conceiving of intuition is Kantian, likewise the insistence on not knowing the nature of things in themselves but their effects. What is different is the appeal to the 'scientific' logic of causality that endorses a new empiricism: 'Your senses mediate the connection between the object and yourselves'. Later, as we will discover, Hegel will criticize Schleiermacher among others for this 'empirical self-consciousness' that fosters a natural religion – albeit of a different kind from the natural religion advocated by eighteenth-century rationalists like Paley. The effect identifies the cause unambiguously, so that Schleiermacher can speak of 'immediate perception' and 'the immediate experiences of the existence and action of the universe'. It is as if intuitions were not blind, but rather were the bearers of a knowledge unmediated by the categories of the understanding and the concepts they furnished. This language of immediacy announces an ontological project alien to Kantian epistemology. It seems to offer an account of a direct apprehension of the way things are such that one can experience the infinite in the finite and so demonstrate the reality of the religious. 'Everything in religion is immediate and true for itself . . . In religion . . . a stronger relationship between intuition and feeling takes place, and intuition never predominates so much that feeling is almost extinguished', he writes. And it is upon this basis that he can confidently proclaim the essence of religion:

> The universe is uninterruptedly active and reveals itself to us at every moment. Every form which is produced, every being to which it gives a separate life in accordance with the fullness of life, every occurrence which it pours out of its rich, ever-fruitful womb, is an action of the universe upon us; and in this way, to accept everything individual as a part of the whole, everything limited as a presentation of the infinite, is religion.

The implications of Schleiermacher's definition of the essence of religion are profound, and when reading any number of nineteenth- and twentieth-century accounts of the nature of religion the reverberations of this tsunami are still discernible. First, this essence installs religion as prior to philosophy, prior to reason. It is not prior to ethics to the extent that, as we will see more clearly in a moment, the content of feeling (a piety issuing from a profound sense of dependency) implies a context in which one is always responsible. Secondly, the essence locates the effective nature of religion in the individual's experience. Only the individual can understand and finally interpret the burden of what is felt. Thirdly, it gives as the content of this religious experience an intuition of oneness with the world, as being a part of a whole, as comprising a finite moment in an infinite extension. Fourthly, in this content the essence of religion is distinguished from a Supreme Being. What God is in God's self remains a mystery; we name 'God' after the effects of this feeling of the infinite. In the passage quoted above, Schleiermacher speaks of the 'universe' as active and revealing itself; the universe giving life; the universe as an 'ever-fruitful womb'. And the universe is then transposed into 'a presentation of the infinite'.

Feeling and intuition, if not exactly identical, are both closely bound up with that crucial verb 'accept' or receive. What is impressed upon us, the religious content of what is accepted or received, is a 'presentation of the infinite' in the contingent and particular. What was once under the jurisdiction of the mystic is now democratized, for mysticism is now the very essence of all true religion. And if religion is the primordial feeling upon the basis of which all other thinking and action proceeds, then Karl Barth is right to observe that what Schleiermacher is telling the cultured despisers is that 'without mysticism there could not be any civilization'. Again, Schleiermacher and the other early Romantics are rethinking Kant. For Kant had made a connection between intuition and the infinite with respect to his understanding of the sublime. The sublime was experienced only in relation to nature and 'Nature is sublime in those of its appearances the intuition of which carries the idea of its infinity in it'. What is significant in the experience of the sublime for the new turn in the understanding of 'religion', as Kant examined it, is its negative power. The 'unfathomability of the idea of freedom' which is received 'completely cuts off any positive representation of it'. The imagination struggles with reason as it strives 'to progress toward infinity'. The understanding is eclipsed and so the 'idea' of the infinite can never be articulated. It is ineffable. Coming before thought and the philosophical, then, this mystical character is pre-rational, possibly irrational. Beyond language and representation it returns us to the limitations and inadequacies of human understanding in an experience of negative pleasure. Nevertheless, although in a footnote in *The Critique of Judgement* he alludes to a similarity between the sublime and the religious, for Kant, religion is concerned with the ethical, with practical reasoning.

It is Schleiermacher and the young Romantics who associate the religious with the sublime, developing, simultaneously, the dynamic capacities of the imagination and the negativity at the heart of the experience. Schleiermacher urges the 'despisers' to 'seek these heavenly sparks that arise when a holy soul is stirred by the universe, and you must overhear them in the incomprehensible moment when they are formed'. The 'infinite chaos' of the starry heavens is related to what is essentially religious. In seeking the infinite the human being experiences the 'silent disappearance of his whole existence in the immeasurable'. Again, as with Novalis, the reintegration with the infinite unity, the One, is the very purpose and operation of religion. To be consumed is the telos of religious desire. The part is assimilated back into the whole, losing its particularity, and a process bound to human eros, imagination and *poiesis* is integrated into a process that is natural – the historical determination of the universe itself. 'Strive here already to annihilate your individuality and to live in the one and the all', Schleiermacher cries, in the final moments of his second lecture.

We need to pause here and make manifest what is distinctive about this Romantic appeal to the negation, or consumption, or immersion, or diremption of self and world. For Christianity has, throughout its history, fostered various forms of self-denial and invested heavily in the apophatic or that which cannot be known or spoken about with respect to God. The character of the mystic and the cataloguing of certain texts under 'mystical writings' only took place in the seventeenth century. Before that, self-denial and approaches to the darkness of God were the practices of 'saints'. Furthermore, these practices were part of a public formation of subjects, or a public disciplining of the soul. The practices were not private. They were conducted in and through liturgies, in and through meditations upon the Bible, and always under the guidance of a superior. The practices took place in monasteries or convents, or other ecclesial communities. The French Jesuit historian, Michel de

Certeau, dates the cultural development of mysticism's relation to private experience from late medieval Catholicism to seventeenth-century 'spirituality'. He also charts the gradual distancing of the personal spiritual guide, and the liturgical/ecclesial setting. The Bible remained a meditative source, but it was now consumed alone, in the privacy of one's chamber and in one's own language.[8] What effect this privatized 'mysticism' had upon early Romanticism is unclear, but evidently the self-abnegation and the entry into the dark infinity in Novalis, Schlegel and Schleiermacher proceeds on a different basis from either the medieval process of sanctity or the seventeenth-century cultivation of the 'spiritual'.

The influence of Spinoza's work is very clear. The monism Spinoza conceived advanced that all things are only modifications of God, the one substance. All difference and distinctiveness were therefore, ultimately, illusion. As each develops intellectually what comes to be understood is that the individual, the singular, the specific and the contingent are all modifications of the one substance. The move towards what Spinoza called 'the intellectual love of God', or the third knowledge, did not require a guide, a liturgical context, nor a sacred text. It was a process that followed from human reasoning itself, but the knowledge of such oneness required the consumption of the one who is knowing, the diremption of reason.

Novalis's admiration for Spinoza is recorded in his letters to Schlegel. He associated Spinoza with one of the fathers of eighteenth-century German Pietism, Count Nikolaus Zinzendorf. For Novalis, Spinoza offered a vision of the profound interpenetration of all things by the whole, such that the human being participates in a cosmic process. The creative freedom of the poet is analogically related to the creative freedom of what Schlegel termed the spirit of universality. Thinking itself becomes divining as it translates the infinite chaos of external phenomena, through the imagination, into an infinite unity. Poetry, as a highest activity of the imagination, discovered what Novalis described as 'the most inward community of finite and infinite'. As such the artistic aspiration fused with the spirit of universality, and a deification of the human was glimpsed. Self-immolation was the nature of artistic endeavour as the presentiment of the infinite demanded the dissolution of the finite individual:

The desire is ever springing,
On the lover to be clinging,
Round him all out spirit flinging,
One with him to be –
Ardent impulse ever heeding
To consume in turn each other,
Only nourished, only feeding,
On each other's ecstasy.

Schlegel could speak of Novalis as 'a new Christ', for the poet mediated the universal love only through his self-sacrifice; only by allowing himself to be consumed as he is consuming. Dedicated to penetrating the infinite, the poet was both the priest at the Catholic mass and the offering. In 'Christianity or Europe' Novalis affirmed his conviction in the 'total capability of all things earthly to be the wine and the bread of eternal life'. What a Spinoza-inspired worldview facilitated, then, for both Schlegel and Novalis, was a final dissolution of the boundaries between religion, philosophy and aesthetics. For poetry and religion were both products of the imagination as philosophy was a reflection upon the operation of the imagination itself. Religion could become another name or what in another mode of discourse might be philosophy or poetry. All was subsumed in the category of 'poesie' or *poiesis*. But the idea of absorption into the one as 'to consume in turn each other' has a darker side – a cannibalism yet to be faced.

Schleiermacher had been educated by the Moravian Brethren founded by Zinzendorf. He tells us that Spinoza 'was full of religion and full of the holy spirit'. He does not add that Spinoza was also Jewish and, as a Jewish philosopher of religion, championed by Moses Mendelssohn. This is important because it gives us a clue as to what remains unresolved in the 1799 edition of *On Religion*. For Spinoza's monism is not, finally, what Schleiermacher is articulating – so Schleiermacher saves himself from the more threatening aspects of dissolution. Tensions were evident in Schleiermacher's relationships with both Novalis and Schlegel. Schleiermacher was disturbed by what seemed to be an account of his ideas given by Novalis in 'Christianity and Europe'. Arguments flared between Schleiermacher and Schlegel. Extensive revisions were made to *On Religion* in subsequent editions (in 1806 and 1821). These tensions, differences and revisions are fundamental for the future development of 'religion' and the re-emergence of a category related to religion but more specifically tied to the practices of the Christian faith: 'theology'.

The second of the lectures in *On Religion* opens itself to – perhaps even offers itself for – misreading. Schleiermacher repeats, on a number of occasions, that he is speaking the language of the 'despisers'. For example, as already noted, Schleiermacher speaks of an immediate relation between the infinite and the finite human being, such that the former consumes the latter. There are moments when the language and thinking seem so close to Schlegel and Novalis one can understand why they could read their own thoughts as in a mirror in that second lecture. The performativity of Schleiermacher's language moves between religious, philosophical and poetic forms of speaking. It is this performativity that confuses the identity of the addressee; for it makes it impossible to be sure in any given set of ideas whether the audience is to understand itself as 'despisers' or disciples. Put in more contemporary literary terms, one is never sure whether the implied reader (the 'you' being addressed) is an insider or an outsider. There are thunderous denunciations of cold moralism and metaphysics that Schlegel and Novalis could only have agreed with, but there are other notes sounded, even in the very context of 'speak[ing] your language', which evidently would be troubling. Let me set out the content of these other notes, for I wish to argue that in *On Religion* Schleiermacher is working towards an account of religion quite at odds with the Romantic conception of religion as a self-dissolving experience of the infinite. Furthermore, the history of 'religion' from *On Religion* to the present has been a playing out of both sides of the distinction that Schleiermacher was struggling to forge.

Five distinctive differences between the religion of Novalis and Schlegel and the religion of Schleiermacher are significant for the new religious project sensed by Schleiermacher, but not fully articulated, until his *magnum opus* of 1821–2, *The Christian Faith*.

First, and perhaps foremost, there remains something of a Kantian resistance to viewing the sensible and the intelligible as 'part of the same infinite continuum',[9] such that the sensible was then consumed

89

by the intelligible which itself was an organ for the infinite unity. Schleiermacher does not accept the Kantian division between the noumenal and the phenomenal that led to a division between the ontological and the epistemological, but Schleiermacher's attention to the pre-reflexive work of the imagination, to the immediate self-consciousness designated by 'feeling', accepted an account of the work of synthetic *a priori* in a Kantian manner. Only Schleiermacher's *a priori* of understanding were not the twelve categories but all the historical particularities of a specific language and a cultural context. For example, there is a moment in the second lecture when he gives an account of what he calls the 'natal hour' of religion:

> That first mysterious moment that occurs in every sensory perception, before intuition and feeling have separated, where sense and its objects have, as it were, flowed into one another and become one, before both turn back to their original position – I know how indescribable it is and how quickly it passes away . . . It is as fleeting and transparent as the first scent with which the dew gently caresses the waking flowers, as modest and delicate as a maiden's kiss, as holy and fruitful as a nuptial embrace . . . I lie on the bosom of the infinite world. At this moment I am its soul, for I feel all its powers and its infinite life as my own; at this moment it is my body, for I penetrate its muscles and its limbs as my own, and its innermost nerves move according to my sense and my presentiment as my own.

Here are the erotics of Novalis's poetry and Schlegel's novel of his relationship with Dorothea (*Lucinda*). Here we also have the interpenetration of finite and infinite. But one observes the casual 'as it were' which introduces the whole account, the self-conscious similitudes 'as the first scent . . . as a nuptial embrace'. The mimetic performance of religion's natal hour is a rhetorical effect. It is not experienced as such outside of its recreation, and Schleiermacher emphasizes this by introducing the passage with a warning: 'the simplest matter separates itself into two opposing elements, the one group combining into an image of an object, the other penetrating to the centre of our being . . . We cannot escape this fate even with the innermost creation of the religious sense; we cannot communicate them except in this separate form.' Understanding and knowledge depend upon articulation and so language inserts itself necessarily ('this fate') into the very mechanisms of reasoning itself. In his later hermeneutical thought, Schleiermacher argues that we never transcend language, and language is always culturally and historically particular.

But this leads to an important question with respect to 'religion' as Schleiermacher understands it. If the pre-reflexive moment is always and only intelligible to us as it is mediated through our words, if this is the nature of 'feeling' understood as unreflected self-consciousness, and if what is given in that feeling is the infinite, then why name this intuition of the transcendent religious? It could be an aesthetic moment (the sublime); it could be a philosophical moment (the first principle or that which is the condition for the possibility of everything else). The infinite dependence, what Schleiermacher when defining God later in his explicitly theological work *The Christian Faith* will term the feeling of absolute dependence, is an inference of there being self-consciousness at all. But why characterize that inference as religious? Why name it as such?

In answering this question we move towards the heart of the debate between Schleiermacher and the early Romantics. Schleiermacher names it as such because he defines his experiences within the context of a specific religious revelation, practice and tradition. That is, for Schleiermacher, we can only name this original moment as religious from within an understanding and knowledge of a particular tradition. The language with which we name this moment is taken from a specific heritage. 'I fear that religion can be understood only through itself and that its special manner of construction and its characteristic distinction will not become clear to you until you yourselves belong to some one or other of them'. This is Schleiermacher's famous hermeneutical circle: what we come to understand is a clarification of what we have already presupposed.

The corollaries of this key distinction for understanding 'religion' are made evident in the other differences between Schleiermacher and the early Romantics. For, on the basis of this hermeneutical account of religious experience, Schleiermacher gropes towards a second distinction: that between religion and the discourses of poetry and philosophy. Schlegel and Novalis integrate the religious into the aesthetic and philosophical intuition of the spirit of universality. But Schleiermacher makes the aesthetic and the philosophical depend upon the more fundamental religious intuition. For religion understands a 'higher unity'. Beyond the intimations of infinity – 'the prodigious masses scattered in that boundless space that runs through immeasurable paths' – lay the more profound intuition of 'divine unity and the eternal immutability of the world'. The moment of the sublime and the infinite are in themselves not religious. 'What actually appeals to the religious sense in the external world is not its masses but its laws.' Again, we must recall, the religious is named as such only on the basis of specific forms of religious practice. These forms enable the identification of religion to be made; the aesthetic and the philosophical then serve the religious, and the religious moment is a realization of a transcendental relation that exceeds the self-transcendence of finite subject encountering the otherness of the world's infinity. Schleiermacher accomplishes here a double distinction important for the history of religion. He distinguishes two forms of infinity: the infinity of the material universe that serves as the 'forecourt' of religion and 'the infinite fullness' of the religious experience of what is higher, framing the material orders. He distinguishes, then, two forms of religion: the natural and the positive. Natural religion is the Spinozist, monist religion of Schlegel and Novalis that 'consists wholly in the negation of everything positive and characteristic in religion', that is everything that gives religion form. The refusal to engage with the specific forms of religion combined with the exultation of a general religious spirituality, Schleiermacher suggests, fails to understand true religion, and therefore fails to understand religion at all.

Hence, Schleiermacher wishes to make a third distinction between this 'true religion' and the spiritualized aestheticism of Schlegel and Novalis. He insists upon the inability to move beyond the materiality of the world. The experience of the infinite is not a translation out of cultural and historical specificities. There is no encounter with the spirit of universality in and of itself. The infinite is always and only located in the finite; particularly in encountering the specific individuality of another person. True religion is always and only a mediated religion. It involves not the losing of identity and the absorption into what is other and infinite, but the fulfilling and development of identity. True religion leads to 'active citizenship in the religious world' and a finer sense of one's own individuality. The sense of one's own humanity is also a sense of what is incomplete about oneself. Dependence upon specific others is therefore foundational for 'the perfect intuition of humanity' as a whole. The heroic individualism of the Romantic artistic genius who mediates the infinite within the finite and often loses the specificity of the sensuous and the social, is countered in Schleiermacher by an appeal to the interpersonal nature of all experience, especially religious experience. Interrelationality is, for him, the basis for self-transcendence and intimations of the infinite. The content of the religious moment is an intuition of interdependency rather that interpenetration.

An understanding of the basis of this interdependency and interrelationality demonstrates, in brief, the operation of different modes of reasoning between Schleiermacher and the early Romantics. For Schlegel and Novalis, following Fichte, to overcome the Kantian divide between the world and the creativity of the reflective subject, a link is forged between the free determination of the I and the Absolute on the basis of longing for the Absolute. The longing is given expression in the philosophical labour of reflection, but the ongoing representation of that longing for the unrepresentable, the *poiesis*, instantiates the co-determinations of the finite I and the infinity of the Absolute. Novalis sums up this sentiment in an observation found in his volume 'Pollen': 'The highest task of *Bildung* is – to gain power over one's transcendental self – to be simultaneously that I of one's I'. The link forged is, simultaneously, an aesthetic and philosophical one. Now Schleiermacher also wishes to overcome the Kantian divide. But his reason for doing so is theological: the Christian account of incarnation (which, for him, is the religious moment at its most profound) announces a compatibility between the finite and the infinite, the human and the divine. The link forged to overcome the Kantian divide is a theological one: an account of the *imago dei*. Schleiermacher ends *On Religion* with an exhortation to worship 'the God within you' and earlier in that final lecture advises the 'despisers' to pay 'heed to how mightily the deity quite specifically edifies even as its holiest and truest . . . the part of the soul in which it preeminently dwells, in which it reveals and contemplates itself in its direct workings'. The God without and infinitely external is also the God within, the apex of the mystery of being human. The universalism of the 'God with you' constitutes the basis for what is universally human in the particularity of each individual. A Christian (more specifically Pietist) understanding of the i*mago dei* drives Schleiermacher's social account of religion, not some universalized form of human reasoning or some universalized form of human creativity.

With Schleiermacher, the Christian character of 'religion' becomes not only evident, but also emphatic. If the mystical is the precondition for the civilized, then with Schleiermacher, as Karl Barth observed, 'Civilization as the triumph of the spirit over nature is the most peculiar work of Christianity'. Schleiermacher was far more conservative and closer to his evangelical father than either Novalis or Schlegel, or perhaps he himself, realized. Although he recognized that religious intuition can take many different particular forms, and each form will depend upon its cultural and historical context, he embraces the new understanding of history as progress. Within a development or evolutionary account of religion, polytheism gives way to monotheism and monotheism reaches its finest expression in Christianity. For Schleiermacher, the 'original intuition of Christianity is more glorious, more sublime, more worthy of adult humanity, more deeply penetrating into the spirit of systematic religion, and extending further over the whole universe'. There are several reasons for this. Primarily, the narrative of the incarnation as the deity's handling of the striving of all things finite both against the unity of the whole (in the defence of individual, 'self-seeking endeavour') and for the infinite, receives its perfect form in Christianity. Consequently, Christianity is a religion founded upon those all-important Romantic notions of mediation and self-reflexivity. Or to put it in Schleiermacher's way: Christianity receives its cultural apotheosis in a reoriented Romanticism. As such, Schleiermacher argues an aspect of Christianity presents itself that makes manifest its perfection: it is able to reflect upon its own practices and other practices. For since Christianity's goal is infinite holiness and it recognizes the operation of 'an irreligious principle', then it unmasks every false morality, every inferior religion and every unfortunate mixture of the two. It is a polemical religion both with respect to the context in which it finds itself and with regard to its own actions. Christianity, then, 'treats religion itself as the material for religion and thus is, as it were, raised to a higher power of religion'.

But this account of Christianity as the complete fulfilment of the religious ideal does not mean that the understanding of 'religion' by Schlegel and Novalis was non-Christian. As we saw in chapter 2, the development of the concept of 'religion' arose in and through the specificities of Christian history and bore all the watermarks of secularized Christian ideals: the brotherhood of 'man', love towards the other, universal peace, the one God, salvation through self-denial and inner conviction of the truth. As the contemporary Islamic ethnographer, Talal Asad, emphasizes: 'It is preeminently the Christian church that has occupied itself with identifying, cultivating and testing belief as a verbalizable inner condition of true religion'.[10] The Christianity in Schlegel's and Novalis's understanding of religion is hidden beneath generalities and philosophical abstractions, such that Schleiermacher believes what he is doing is giving that religion its necessary, concrete expression. The act of persuasion he is performing presupposes, above and beyond institutions and formal moral principles, that the 'despisers' will recognize the Christianity implicit in their understanding of religion as in his. Interestingly, for the way he rejects Judaism on the grounds that it is an historical anachronism, he employs the image of the temple to map the positions of the natural religionists. They occupy a place in the forecourt, but he wishes to bring them into the Holy of Holies, the *sanctum sanctorum*. In fact, Schlegel's wife Dorothea did follow Schleiermacher's directions, as also did Novalis. Though both of them moved more distinctly in a Roman Catholic direction, Schlegel himself baulked at the return to the specificities of Christianity and found the final lecture unpalatable. Nevertheless, for the story we are telling, what remains significant is the way Schleiermacher points up the dangers of the general or natural account of religion. Its dangers, as he observes them, consist in its espousal of negation.[11] He does not use the word 'nihilism', but in delineating its emptiness, its indeterminate form and its 'merely loose, unrelated material', he draws attention to the way in which this understanding of religion seeks transcendence in the chaotic, the indifferent, the contentless, the 'empty spaces' of the 'human personality'.

Schleiermacher goes no further but, as we will see, Herman Melville explores the religion that is preoccupied with the void.

This refusal to endorse a religious naturalism, the fourth of the distinctions between Schleiermacher and the young Romantics, and this appeal to what might be called the materialist dialectic between the finite and the infinite, led to the development of a split in the construal of 'religion'. In *On Religion* Schleiermacher employs the term 'positive religion', as we have seen. But in later revisions of the work he writes of 'the confusion between religion and the know-ledge which belongs to theology' (1806) and he begins to speak of 'the knowledge of God'. Richard Crouter, the English editor and translator of the 1799 edition of *On Religion*, observes: 'In 1799 the term "theology" actually occurs only once, in a pejorative reference to "systems of theology"; and "knowledge of God" never occurs in the 1806'.[12] Ironically, given Karl Barth's attack on Schleiermacher's work for its cultural accommodationism, it is Schleiermacher who reintroduces the idea of 'theology' as a distinctive mode of discourse and tradition-based knowledge. Concerning this idea and its appeal to tradition and rejection of modernity's secularism, we will have more to say in chapter 4. What is significant here is that under religious naturalism Schleiermacher refers to both Enlightenment theism and Romantic pantheism. He makes no distinction between them for they both trade on emptiness – the first formally and the second experientially.

It is in this context that the fifth and final distinction can be recognized. Schleiermacher avoids the language of Dionysian ecstasy that both Schlegel and Novalis entertain and encourage. For Dionysius is associated with the night, the erotic, the Eleusinian mysteries and the important Romantic principle of liberation through negation, death or dissolution. In his 1797 essay 'On the Study of Greek Literature' Schlegel already invokes the difference between the aes-thetics of Dionysius and the aesthetics of Apollo made famous later by Nietzsche. He speaks of the 'divine intoxication of Dionysius'. Romantic art was energized by the creative destructions of this Greek deity. But this is not the nature of religious feelings for Schleiermacher, which are characterized by the way they 'inhibit the strength of our action and invite us to calm and dedicated enjoyment'. Here is not ecstasy but piety, the even-tempered instilling of 'serenity and rest'. It is, on the contrary, 'evil spirits, not good ones, [that] possess a person and drive him'. The language of possession, of enthusiasm, of inspiration (in German, *Begeister*) is important to the quasi-messianic and prophetic roles the early Romantics forge for themselves as artists. But again Schleiermacher hints at the dangers of understanding these operations and dynamics as religious intuitions; the dangers of *poeisis* so conceived that conflates transcendence with aesthetics and philosophical speculation. The interpretative labour he wrote of later in his *Hermeneutics* is the counterbalance to the breakdown and overthrow of reason threatened by thirst for the infinite. The systematic account of Christian doctrine as it emerges as the expression of the religious intuition, developed in *The Christian Faith*, stands as a counterweight to the Romantic rhetorics of sublime excess and death as the fulfilment of love as desire.

With Schleiermacher there is both an account of the essence of religion and the beginning of a counter-trend to such universalism. But as Karl Barth charted in his exhaustive account of *Protestant Theology in the Nineteenth Century*, it was not Schleiermacher's counter-trend that prevailed. Rather, what developed – and Barth blamed Schleiermacher ironically for it – was the alliance between the religious and the mystical experience of self-annihilation, from the subjective point of view, and an account of religion itself as a symbolic system, from the objective point of view. Both of these developments come together in G. W. F. Hegel's transformation of the Good Friday event of the death of God into world history.

The Mediation of Death

Although Hegel was brought up in the Lutheran tradition, studied at the Protestant seminary at Tübingen and composed a number of early essays on theological themes, his lecture courses on the philosophy of religion belong to the later period of his life. In 1807 he had published some of his ideas on the relationship between religion, representation and philosophy in his staggeringly suggestive *Phenomenology of Spirit*. But it was not until 1821, when he was Professor of Philosophy at the University of Berlin, that Hegel began to construct what only one person before him (a former student) had consciously attempted, a philosophy of religion. Schleiermacher, who held a Chair of Theology at the same university, had much to do with this new departure. For Schleiermacher was preparing to publish that year his major work, *The Christian Faith*. This book attempted to think Christian doctrine through systematically on the basis that God named that foundational feeling of absolute dependence.

Hegel's relationship with Schleiermacher while at Berlin was not an easy one. Schleiermacher had accepted Hegel's appointment at Berlin unenthusiastically and prevented Hegel from ever being elected to the prestigious (and financially beneficial) Berlin Academy of Sciences. What Schleiermacher took exception to was the 'speculative' philosophy that Hegel was developing – that is, reflection upon reflection itself. He, among several others, did not view this as a 'science'. Hegel, for his part, was always opposed to 'positive' religion and did not think highly of Schleiermacher's theology of feeling. In the mid-1790s he had written an (unpublished) essay entitled 'Positivity' attacking religion based on ecclesial authority and arguing that Christianity itself had become unintentionally a 'positive' religion only under various cultural pressures following Christ's death. He continued to advocate what he first called a 'people's religion', closely linked, as with the Greek *polis*, with the workings of the state. Furthermore, as a category for reflection 'feeling' lacked the rigour of logical reasoning that was so important for Hegel's view of the world, its history and its teleology. He published his critique against this view of religion founded upon feeling in 1821 in the preface to a book by a former student on the philosophy of religion. Here he referred first to Schlegel (by name) as being a first-rate representative of the 'evils of our time' and then to Schleiermacher (not by name): 'if religion grounds itself in a person only on the basis of feeling, then such a feeling would have no other determination than that of a *feeling of his dependence*, and so a dog would be the best Christian, for it carries this feeling most intensely within itself and lives principally in this feeling'. It is not that Hegel found no place for feeling in religion, but he accepted the classical distinction that what distinguished human beings from animals was the ability to think, and it was a consequence of this ability to think that human beings alone had religion. Feeling, even understood as immediate self-consciousness, could not then be the founding principle of religion. So what did religion base itself upon? Hegel's answer might seem highly orthodox from a Christian perspective (and Hegel, like Schleiermacher, saw Christianity as the absolute or consummate religion): the origin of religion was God's own self-revelation.

In expounding the nature of this self-revelation we can appreciate how profoundly Hegel's conception of religion is dictated by the Christian doctrine of the trinity. In fact, the whole of Hegel's philosophical and political thinking is dictated by the threefold operation in which the absolute idea (God) realizes itself. Its first mode of being is substantial self-unity (God as father); its second mode of being is its self-differentiation (God as incarnate Son); and its third mode of being is its self-consummation (God as Spirit), where the universal – having become the particular – returns to itself as God's self-consciousness of his own singularity. Since, for Hegel, all consciousness participates in the movement of God's self-consciousness, then all thinking and reflection ultimately has as its goal the realization of God.

The Christian doctrine of the trinity is the deep structure for Hegel's account of how we know anything. Hence, it is not feeling which is the fundamental origin of our notion of religion, but thinking or self-reflection. The origin and telos, then, of both religion and philosophy is the same – God's self-realization – such that religion is not a human construction without also, simultaneously, being a particularization of the divine. And so, in a move that recalls the early Romantics, 'Philosophy is only explicating *itself* when it explicates religion, and when it explicates itself it is explicating religion'. The circulating style is a characteristic of Hegel's notoriously difficult prose, but the circulations are highly important, for they draw us into the dialectical nature of Hegel's thinking (and, for Hegel, all thinking). There is no final, static position. Every position is in transit and about to cross over into a further self-reflection, a further negotiation with that which is outside the subject. Therefore, before concluding that Hegel conflates philosophy and religion, it must be emphasized that the Christian faith provides the framework for the unification of these two modes of approaching

God. But – and here comes the circularity again – it is philosophy which demonstrates through a 'logical exposition' that 'this idea [of the trinity] is what is true as such, and that all categories of thought are this movement of determining'.

There is much that is both complex and interesting about Hegel's philosophical understanding of religion or his religious understanding of philosophy. The ground has been debated and fought over by any number of scholars, and the received ideas about the nature of dialectical movement towards the realization of the absolute and its relationship to theology has, in recent times, been the subject of a number of 'revisions' of Hegel.[13] For the argument of this book three points are salient.

First, the universalization of religion is, with Hegel as with Schleiermacher, founded upon the teachings of the Christian faith. In fact, the trinitarian grammar of Hegel's thinking, and thinking as such, roots religion more firmly in Christianity than Schleiermacher's distinction between the immediate feeling of absolute dependence and the mediated forms that such a feeling takes.[14] In other words, Schleiermacher is working with a Kantian dualism between the immediate and the mediated such that feeling is pre-reflexive. Hegel, on the other hand, can have no pre-reflexive moment. The immediate intuition already has cognitive content because it participates is a threefold act of self-cognition above and beyond the human: 'in [human] spirit as such the consciousness of God is immediately present along with consciousness of itself'. If the immediate intuition has cognitive content it follows that something can be known about God's own self. In his *Dialectics* Schleiermacher states that 'we only know about the being of God in us and in things. We know nothing whatever about a being of God outside the world or in himself'. Hegel would agree that we know nothing of God outside the world, but nevertheless God in himself can be known because of the profound relation between the operation of human consciousness or spirit and the operation of God's own consciousness or absolute spirit. But the trinitarian grammar of God's own consciousness has to be logically – that is philosophically – explicated and so philosophy of religion becomes the most foundational branch of philosophy as such. Philosophy enables religion to reflect upon itself and arrive at a higher understanding of its own divine basis. This move towards a higher abstraction Hegel calls 'sublation'. There is a sublation then of the specifically religious by the philosophical. Only on this basis can there develop, for Hegel, a 'science of religion'; and what his philosophy of religion is attempting to provide is a basis for the scientific study of religion. It is his work that lays the basis for religious studies as an academic discipline pursued within the university.

Nevertheless, secondly, despite the sublation, the self-realization of God requires determinative expression. And in explicating the types of expression, Hegel is one of the first to provide us with a map of world religions. Schleiermacher is vague on other religions outside Judaism and Christianity, polytheism and monotheism; his world remains Classical and Western in scope. But in the second section of his *Lectures on the Philosophy of Religion* Hegel travelled intellectually beyond his Classical and Western mind-set, collating as much information as was available to him to construct a typology of religious practices past and present. The account he gives is, like Schleiermacher's, developmental – towards Christianity as the absolute religion. But it is development not simply along a diachronic axis, but also a synchronic axis. That is, while viewing religion as evolving historically from natural forms, through forms in which an elevation of the spiritual over the natural is evident, to the Roman religion of expediency and, finally, Christian trinitarianism, Hegel also views religions as evolving rationally. In their rational development, religions move from beliefs and practices founded upon sensible immediacy or 'empirical self-consciousness' to those beliefs and practices in which the absolute indeterminacy of the One is incarnated in the particularity of Christ and through the operation of the spirit of Christ in, through and with the spirituality of human beings, returns to God as absolute substance. With this double account of the historical evolution and the logical elevation, then, Christianity as the consummate form of religion is found partially fulfilled in other forms of religious beliefs and practices. In other words, rather than Schleiermacher's dismissive view of other religions (Judaism particularly) as no longer relevant, with Hegel we have an account of religious pluralism. For he recognizes not only that many of the religions he describes are still being practised, but that Buddhism 'is the most widespread religion on earth . . . The people adhering to

101

this religion are more numerous than the Muslims, as the Muslims in turn are more numerous than the Christians'. So while Christianity is superior in terms of both its historical and its logical development of the absolute idea, Hegel's global comprehensiveness offers, for the first time, recognition of the integrity of other faith systems.[15] Speaking of Buddhism, which, as we shall see, Hegel was very interested in, he writes: 'It is easy to say that such a religion is just senseless and irrational. What is not easy to recognize is the necessity and truth of such religious forms, their connection with reason.' Of course, there is only one form of reason – that which is triadic and ultimately based upon the logic of the syllogism – and all religions are examined with respect to how adequately they articulate this one reason. Nevertheless, Hegel provides a sophisticated philosophical method for investigating the religiously pluralistic world in which he sees Christianity participating. Furthermore, ultimately all religions have the same goal: the self-realization of the absolute and indeterminate. God as the one absolute and indeterminate substance is the final reality of 'all higher religions, but particularly in the Christian religion'.

It is important to recognize the philosophical basis upon which all these religions can be compared. We are returned to the priority that Hegel gives to the philosophical and to that tension between logically requiring and indeed emphasizing the determinate and the particular, while also logically requiring and emphasizing the need to sublate the particular, in order to make manifest the operation of the logic itself. The finite and material can easily be understood as the vehicle for or container of the infinite and spiritual.

The story of Adam and Eve, for example, can be viewed as containing 'the essential or basic features of the idea', the idea being 'portrayed mythically in the mode of a temporal process'. In other words the philosophical method requires a methodological distinction to be made between the idea and its mediation or representation. The philosophical demythologizes such that the concrete can appear as so much cultural symbolic clothing. This peeling back of the particular to reach the transhistorical and transcultural core will become, following Hegel, an important method in the exegesis of biblical texts. On the basis of this process, Hegel's pupil David Friedrich Strauss will examine the life of Jesus and provoke one of the most far-reaching theological controversies of the nineteenth century. In the early twentieth century the theologian Rudolph Bultmann will explore the difference between the mythological and the *kerygmatic* in the New Testament, and the much later twentieth-century debates of the *Myth of God Incarnate* rest upon the credibility of such a distinction.

For Hegel, the fundamental law of sublation or elevation requires an equally fundamental principle of negation. The negative becomes the mediating term in the return to the one substance. Hegel draws close here to the operation of the negative in Novalis and Schlegel. Once more death, sacrifice and renunciation of the natural and finite are fundamental religious moments. But Hegel now locates these moments within God's own self-development, the transcendental trinity as it is chronicled historically in the life of Jesus Christ. In Christ, 'Death, the negative, is the mediating term through which the original majesty is posited as now achieved'.

We need now to examine this process of negation more closely in order to understand the new relations this began to forge between religion, the Void and the death of God. This is the third of the salient points to be made about religion as Hegel understood and determined it. There are two philosophical words used by Hegel to bear this character of negation: sublation (or the stripping away of the finite and determinate in an elevation towards a reflection upon the conceptual or logical) and diremption (or separation whereby there is the establishment of what is other and therefore the negation of the self-same). These philosophical words are related to two particular narratives: that of the Fall (when human beings withdrew from what immediately immersed them into self-consciousness or reflective thought) and that of the coming of the kingdom of God through the sacrifice of Christ. The philosophical vocabulary finds its theological representation in 'Fall' and 'sacrifice', for throughout (as we have seen) philosophy is a higher way of grasping the object of religion itself: the spirit or 'consciousness relating itself to its essence, knowing itself as its essence and knowing its essence as its own'. As such, the death of God as the negation required by the absolute to become external to itself is a necessary moment for that return to 'knowing its essence as its own'. As Hegel puts it (rendering the Christ event universal and History the history of the unfolding of the absolute idea): 'The death of Christ is the midpoint upon which consciousness turns'. Of course, in a sense, the death of God (Christ being the determinate revelation of God as absolute idea) brings about the death of death, for God returns to God's self, is reconciled to God's self. But that negation of negation and the reconciliation of God with what is other than God, the world as that created other to God, only takes place on a speculative plain grasped by faith. On the more mundane and individual plain, human beings are caught between the endless sublation of the natural, the empirical and immediate, a sublation Hegel terms sacrifice, and the immersion, through this sublation, of the finite with the infinite, the determinate with the indeterminate. While we think at all, we necessarily have to think in finite, determinate representations that participate in and make manifest God's own self-consciousness. But God in God's self is an ungraspable, inconceivable 'tranquil mystery'. The three moments are one and 'it is as totality that God is the Spirit'. We necessarily work 'in representational fashion' and so we speak of God as father and Christ as son which is 'only figurative and accordingly never wholly corresponds to what should be expressed'. As Hegel observes, with respect to what he finds true in Buddhism, 'The One is the indeterminate ... what is wholly empty'. He adds, with respect to Christian trinitarianism, 'Unless three determinations are recognized in God, "God" is an empty word'. But the difficulty is the privilege given by Hegel's philosophical orientation to the abstract, so that although, from his Christian perspective, Hegel would understand that God eternally contemplates his relation to the world through Christ, Hegel can only conceive the content of that reflection in abstractions like 'three determinations'. Furthermore, the telos of any individual's thinking is immersion in God-consciousness, the negation of finitude. The consummate religion 'poses the demand that one should remove oneself from finite things and elevate oneself to an infinite energy for which all other bonds are to become matters of indifference'.

Once more we are close to Novalis's understanding of Christianity as the religion of negation, or consumption. And, once more, associated with the endless and necessary sacrifice, the dark figure of cannibalism haunts the imagination. Hegel's most graphic and dramatic writing in the *Lectures* is a depiction of the religion of the Jaga tribe 'from the south of Africa, from the Congo'. Here a witch-doctor

> states that he needs two human beings who must be sacrificed, and designates them from the bystanders, takes a knife, stabs them, drinks their blood, distributes their pieces among the bystanders, and the whole company devours their flesh. Such blood sacrifices are common. It is recounted of that queen of the Jaga that, in order to be strong in war, she pounded her own son in a mortar and, in company with her female companions, devoured his flesh and drank his blood.

What becomes clear here, in a way that does not with Novalis's 'cannibalism', is that the cannibal act is the mirror side of the Christian account of atonement remembered in each eucharistic celebration. The negation and consumption takes on a particularity, a literalness, that is the dark figuring that, for Hegel, Christianity will bring to its redemptive consummation. Indeed, Hegel states that the 'kingdom of God, the new religion, thus contains implicitly the characteristic of negating the present world'. But in order to exorcise the demon of cannibalism, the content of Christianity as 'the true religion' and the logic of its truth moves inexorably towards the abstract, the infinite, the indeterminate and the collapse of the figurative and the representational.

With Hegel we are on the brink of the implosion of 'religion'. For true religion is implicated in an endless self-sublation whereby the specific cultural and historical representation of an idea is, ultimately, viewed as a symbolic carrier for a more profound logic of sacrifice than that of the queen of the Jaga. This implosion of the idea of religion is ironic given that part of Hegel's achievement was the founding of religion as a subject of scientific interest, developing its own rational methodologies and gaining university recognition. But well before Nietzsche's famous reinterpretation of Hegel's 'death of God' thesis, Frederick Engels, a friend of David Friedrich Strauss, could write to Marx in 1844: 'All the possibilities of religion are exhausted'. That exhaustion which Engels described as coming 'after the absolute and abstract religion, after religion "as such"', could provoke two different post-Christian responses: the advocacy of secular materialism and atheism, on the one hand, and the appeal to a transcendental emptiness, a *mysterium tremendum et fascinans* that is ultimately an experience of the unpresentable, on the other. Only the thin thread of threeness maintains the logic of Hegel's religion in the rational, what he would frequently describe as 'the soil of thinking'. When the trinitarian thread is cut religion floats like a ship adrift on the waters of infinity, meditating on extremity.

Religion and the Void: White Ecstasy

Herman Melville captures this new understanding of religion in his epic of 1851, *Moby Dick*, for the whaling ship, the *Pequod*, is crowded with a host of religious fools. The 'good Presbyterian' narrator, who asks to be called 'Ishmael' (after Abraham's first-born), with his pagan idol-worshipping friend, Queequeg, embark on a journey having been warned of its consequences by a prophet Elijah, and welcomed on board by Captain Bildad, the name of one of Job's 'comforters'. They join a crew drawn from around the world, and drawn, by analogy, into the context of that world's religions. Queequeg's pagan fastings and prostrations are described in terms of the Muslim festival of Ramadan; Ahab (the name of an early Israelite king deceived into idolatry by false prophets) is likened to Belshazzar, king of Babylon; the white-turbaned old man, Fedullah, is a Parsee, a Zoroastrian (a dualist); there are references to Persian fire worshippers, sacrifices by the Iroquois, reincarnation, and the Greek Fates. Learned articles have been written on the novel as the incarnation of Egyptian mythology, and the Fish as a manifestation of the Hindu deity Vishnu. The ship is stocked with pious men, because 'as everyone knows, meditation and water are wedded for ever' and 'in landlessness alone resides the highest truth, shoreless, indefinite as God'. And the writing itself, rich in allusion, groans like the ship under the weight of its cosmic and encyclopedic symbolism as it leaves Nantucket on Christmas morning to sink beneath equatorial waters on 'the third day' – consumed by the work of the great white whale.

106

The narrative is framed by the Christian gospel. The prose recites and refers to books from the Old Testament which have been read typologically by the Christian tradition as speaking of Christ: Genesis, Jonah, Job and Isaiah particularly. These references and interpolations are often part of a sinister and sardonic irony – like the liturgy of preaching in which the story of Jonah is expounded, followed and counterpointed by the pagan worship of Queequeg's idol. Nevertheless, Christian mythoi and symbolism inform all levels of the novel's action, even when interlaced with references to other rites and pieties. Both Ahab and Ishmael are wrestling with Christian or Christian-inspired theistic notions of God – though their scathing irony announce post-Christian positions. The other religions are circumscribed within this frame. Ishmael affirms 'the greatest respect towards everybody's religious obligations, never mind how comical, and could not find it in my heart to undervalue even a congregation of ants worshipping a toadstool'. But the final clause hints at an ironic vision related to this 'respect'; the hauteur of the one doing the respecting. Ishmael observes, following Queequeg's fast, that 'he no doubt thought he knew a good deal more about the true religion than I did. He looked at me with a sort of condescending concern and compassion, as though he thought it a great pity that such a sensible young man should be so hopelessly lost to evangelical pagan piety.' But Queequeg only has a voice in so far as the narrator (and the author) gives it to him.

The narrator's post-Christian hauteur, like Ahab's, is at odds with the God who is the 'centre and circumference of all democracy'. The *Pequod*, cargoed with the world's cultural heritage, intellectual and spiritual, is a stage for everyman, and the haunting and the hunting of Moby Dick level each of the sailors. An otherness, an alienation, consumes them inwardly as they bow beneath the monomaniac will and desire of Captain Ahab. They must either subjugate or be subjugated by this sublime immensity, 'not only ubiquitous, but immortal'.

It is the whiteness of the whale which most appals and fascinates. The 'incantation of this whiteness . . . is at once the most meaningful symbol of spiritual things, nay, the very veil of the Christian's Deity; and yet should be as it is, the intensifying agent in things the most appalling to mankind'. Its vast presence beneath the surface of the visible world opens up a profound vulnerability in those who are isolated in remote waters, bound in a wooden shell that is at times their ark and, finally, their coffin. Detached from the concreteness of place, the ship sails upon a permeable line between the finite and the infinite, the natural and the supernatural, things visible and things mystical. The white whale provokes a religiousness that renders all the different practices of piety among the sailors so much super-stition. For beneath what Schleiermacher and Hegel would call the positivity of religions 'thou beholdest even in a dumb brute, the instinct of the knowledge of the demonism in the world'. Moby Dick presents each sailor with an intimation not only of his own mortality. Melville notes that Leviathan is a Hebrew symbol of the chaotic and a Christian symbol of the demonic, but the whale is also the *anima mundi* itself: the Spirit informing all things. Encountering the sperm whale, hunting it down – being driven to hunt it down – invokes an experience of the numinous and the predestined, what Rudolph Otto would call the experience of the holy, the *mysterium tremendum et fascinans*.[16] It is a mystical experience that continually threatens to consume or immerse them.

While Melville dramatizes this consumption quite literally at the end of the novel, the spiritual consumption begins much earlier with the first of several syncretistic liturgies. The crew, each wrapped in his own reflections, participates in a rite both pagan and Christian in which Ahab binds them to the quest for Moby Dick. There, in a bacchanalian scene shot through with references to the papacy and the eucharistic mass, Ahab's obsessive passion is internalized by the others: 'A wild, mystical sympathetical feeling was in me; Ahab's quenchless feud seemed mine'. But then Ahab's passion is never just his own, for as high priest he mediates 'an elemental strife', the badge of his office being the branding that ran from 'crown to sole'. He is both Christ ('with a crucifixion in his face') and Satan ('an infinity of firmest fortitude, a determinate, unsurrenderable wilful-ness'). Like the whale, the ship and the text itself Ahab is symbolic-ally overdetermined. He is consumed by the power of language itself.

Consumption is a significant theme throughout the novel. As with every detail – Ishmael, the cabin table, the smithy, the cistern and buckets and the triple-masted ship – consumption is figured on

108

various levels. There is the international consumption of oil (and perfume) providing the economic structure for the plot. There is the consumption of food – like Mrs Hussey's chowder and Stubb's feasting on the whale's penis. There are also ritual forms of consumption (and fasting) that imitate religious rites. But of all these forms of consuming, the allusions to cannibalism parallel the horror inspired by the whale itself. The cannibalism is introduced early into the narrative with Ishmael's first encounters with Queequeg of the filed and pointed teeth and 'cannibal propensity'. The other stories we hear of Queequeg, the cannibal, show us a man of royal blood and priestly caste. The cannibalism is ritualized. Ahab too, we are told, had been ''mong cannibals'. Ishmael, assuming a New Testament elevation and a rhetoric that is associated with Christ, conflates two forms of consumption: cannibalism and capitalism: 'Cannibals? who is not a cannibal? I tell you it will be more tolerable for the Fejee that salted down a lean missionary in his cellar against a coming famine; it will be more tolerable for that provident Fejee, I say, in the day of judgement, than for thee, civilized and enlightened gourmand, who nailest geese to the ground and feastest on the bloated livers of thy pate-de-fois-gras'. Cannibalism is linked to capitalism through religion – the 'lean missionary', the Christ-like passing of judgement: the three concerns cannot be separated.

One of Melville's main sources for the book was an account of the sinking of the *Essex* in 1821 by an enraged sperm whale. Only what horrified those who heard the reports was not that the ship sank but that the twenty men who escaped the sinking survived only by feeding off the corpses of their friends and colleagues. As the maritime historian Nathaniel Philbrick observes, in his recent retelling of the story of the men who escaped, Melville's novel ends where the story of the *Essex* disaster begins.[17] Melville chooses to focus the consumption theme in the plot not on the men, but on the infinite appetite of the whale obsessing the men. The whale drives them beyond ordinary satisfactions. The cannibalism is made cosmic and divine. The whale's appetite is akin to God's. In a dramatic scene in which the three masts are topped with fire and burn like 'three gigantic wax tapers before an altar', Ahab testifies to the 'clear spirit, to whom all eternity is but time', 'Thou canst consume', and finally utters words which take us back through

109

Hegel to Novalis: 'I burn with thee; would fain be welded with thee'. To be consumed is to have one's life consummated.

This interrelationship between consumption and consummation takes dramatic form when Tashego falls through the head of a captured whale into a pool of the precious (because most pure) spermaceti. The sperm whale gets it name from the great reservoir of milky liquid contained in the whale's head, which resembles seminal fluid. (Hence the facetious irony of calling the white whale Moby Dick.) Since semen is the source of life – sexual difference and the female contribution to the reproductive process were still under investigation when Melville was writing – when the seaman Tashego plummets into a pool of 'semen' and is saved by Queequeg, Melville makes the most of this second birth. Immersed in a seminal fluid, it is the 'obstetrics of Queequeg' that delivers him. But this birthing is subsequent, as all birthing is subsequent, to a consummation. 'Now had Tashego perished in that head, it had been a very precious perishing; smothered in the very whitest and daintiest of fragrant spermaceti; coffined, hearsed, and tombed in the secret inner chamber and sanctum sanctorum of the whale'. Death, mystical union in the holy of holies, consummating orgasm and immersion are inextricable from this white ecstasy.

While Moby Dick does literally consume parts of boats and the limbs of human beings, the whiteness of the whale figures a mystical incorporation:

Is it by its indefiniteness it shadows forth the heartless voids and immensities of the universe, and thus stabs us from behind with the thought of annihilation, when beholding the white depths of the milky way? Or is it that as an essence whiteness is not so much a color as the visible absence of color, and at the same time the concrete of all colors; is it for these reasons that there is such a dumb blankness, full of meaning, in a wide landscape of snows – a colorless, all–color of atheism from which we shrink ? . . . pondering all this, the palsied universe lies before us a leper; and like wilful travellers in Lapland, who refuse to wear colored and coloring glasses upon their eyes, so the wretched infidel gazes himself blind at the monumental white shroud that wraps all the prospect around him.

Here again the religious and the necrophiliac come together in an experience that is at once 'full of meaning' and atheistic, the essence of colour and colourless. 'Heartless voids' and the 'thought of annihilation' take on cosmic and mystical connotations, as the overwhelming experience of light becomes an experience of the most profound absence and blindness. The passage moves from a contemplation of the universe, the invocation of an indeterminate theology and a meditation upon the physics of light to a similitude drawn between 'travellers in Lapland' and 'the wretched infidel' consumed by the light around him. And it is in this very movement that we discern a certain derangement in the prose. For the plural 'travellers' becomes the singular 'infidel' and there is no obvious reason why, in the 'white depths', we should encounter an infidel or why this infidel should be described as 'wretched'. 'Infidel' is one of Ishmael's common epithets, which is ironic in that Ishmael was, by tradition, the father of the Muslim nations and it is the Arab Muslims who were first named the infidel by the Christian church at the time of the Crusades. But then it is the irony, along with the overdetermined allegorization, that signals and orchestrates the derangement.

The irony and the allegory threaten to overthrow the novel itself as a form of communication. Each are means of sublating or negating the given, the meaningful. Working together they undermine any single worldview. At times the dominating vision is Manichaean and dualistic, at times Calvinist; at times a gospel of love and salvation seem to be offered, at times the vitriolic anger becomes demonic and anti-Christian. Critics have floundered in their attempts to unravel the complexity of tone, style and narration and present a unified meaning. But the text, like the *Pequod*, is not stable; it participates in a derangement operating on numerous levels. The inscrutability of God in *Moby Dick* renders all reasoning vulnerable. Frequently, the minds of the men on board the ship are overthrown – with panic, with fear, with hysteria, with joy, with awe, with ecstasy. Madness too becomes another form of immersion, as the little negro boy, Pip, portrays: 'The sea had jeeringly kept his finite body up, but drowned the infinite of his soul. Not drowned entirely, though. Rather carried down alive to wonderous depths.' Madness and death are inseparable aspects of the pursuit of the

111

infinite; they are experiences waiting in the shadows of mystical encounters and consummations. The irony and allegorization provoke a semiosis, an infinite play of meaning, tone and identity, within the novel. Irony, symbolism and word-play ricochet throughout the story, upsetting and unsettling any final appreciation of what is being said. They operate a negation so far-reaching that the will of the Promethean subject – Ahab's, Ishmael's, Melville's – is driven towards a Dionysian vortex, what Ishmael describes as 'that howling infinite'. If the novel is a tragedy, it is a tragedy self-generated, but the reader does not know if the action is tragic. For the reader, while taking in *what* has happened, cannot determine the *meaning* of what has happened sufficient to say whether the story narrates the tragic fall of a modern hero or the fulfilment of a monomaniac's self-destructive fantasies. Is the goodness of God vindicated against the wicked blasphemy of Ahab or is a new heroics born from the very futility of a human being standing up against the malice and tyranny of the Absolute?

What is evident is that religion as the mystical experience of the infinite, as a universal and private experience, fosters a detachment from the quotidian – from the land and the materiality associated with the earth – while valorizing a profound subjugation. Religion so conceived lends imperialism a mystical core: the ubiquity of God invokes a deity of domination. Ahab has been read as a representation of American global desires, its consuming drive to conquest.[18] But then the German metaphysics we have been exploring in this chapter, and its reevaluation of religion, has been used recently to advocate the end of history and the international triumph of liberal democracy through global trade.[19] Hegel's Spirit has been read as the spirit of capitalism. The sublime – its aesthetics and mystics – had political, economic and geographical coordinates: the Alps and the stars for Ruskin; tracks of uncharted territory in Africa and Australia, later in the Arctic and Antarctic; the imperial ambitions of Britain and France, later Germany. The man Hegel most stood in awe of was Napoleon.

In introducing Melville at this point there surfaces what the culture critic Raymond Williams termed 'structures of feeling' as these emerge from the circulation of signs constituting cultural horizons and their transformation. The changes to the understanding of 'religion' represented in *Moby Dick* find certain correlations in the political, the economic, the aesthetic, the metaphysical and the spiritual. The momentous growth in consumer culture that began in the nineteenth century paralleled the new Smithian economics of free trade and the avaricious drive for conquest, are reflected back in the fears, fascinations and figurations of 'religion', the turns to cosmotheism, the Romantic metaphysics of the absolute spirit, the deity who dominates, and the aesthetics of the sublime. A series of related words cross and recross these various discourses: 'consume', 'consummate', 'consumer' (we might even add the medical discourse on consumption). This Promethean will, commanding and indomitable, is driven and haunted by a lack as infinite as it is unappeasable. The obsession is death-bound and mad with an absence it can only surrender itself to. The vast circulation of social energies, within which a new mystical understanding of religion was formed, resembled the whirlpool at the heart of Poe's story *A Descent into the Maelstrom*, the energy storm into which Turner's steam engine is dissolving or the 'yawning gulf' that swallowed the *Pequod*. We stand at the edge of the apocalyptic. Religion peers into the primeval chaos.[20] Chaos is the beginning to which, in the great Romantic circles, we return; a beginning that began, so the biblicalists calculated, five thousand years ago.

Ishmael records, as the *Pequod* goes under: 'Now small fowls flew screaming over the yet yawning gulf; a sullen white surf beat against its steep sides; then all collapsed, and the great shroud of the sea rolled on as it rolled five thousand ago'.

113

4

True Religion as Special Effect

Of course, not everyone on the *Pequod* entered the vortex of the void. Ishmael survives. Though his decision to go whaling is a suicidal one, indicating that he too wished to wrestle with the dominions of death, he is returned to the world. The return enables him to tell the tale. The kind of salvation his survival signifies is frequently debated, but I would argue that he survives *only* to tell the tale – like the ancient mariner – and to tell it over and over again as each new reader encounters the story. In other words, the salvation from ultimate mystical consummation is vouchsafed through art; in this case narrative art. Ishmael mirrors Ahab's dark spiritual drive but does not fall prey to it because he narrates. Ishmael sees his own other – Queequeg, Starbuck, Dough-Boy, etc. – and weaves them into a seamless whole. In the *Birth of Tragedy* Nietzsche writes: 'the sublime . . . subjugates terror by the means of art'. Art becomes the necessary supplement to 'religion' so conceived: it makes the ineffable not only effable but bearable. When the 'howling infinite' of the numinous would negate everything, art alone maintains value. Art alone provides the values and the forms that, while giving access to the numinous, resist its final, seductive subjugation. The aesthetic alone becomes redemptive.

With this we approach the worldview of Baz Luhrmann's *Romeo & Juliet* and the postmodern understanding of religion. But one more significant development in the logic of 'religion' needs to be made concerning value as it relates to religion and art: the move to the commodification of value, in which value is linked to lifestyle and fashion and where freedom, understood as infinite desire, becomes primarily not a mystical but an economic drive. As D. Stephen Long has recently observed, 'non-confessional theology has the same shape as the formal but contentless character of global capitalism. It recognizes 'value', but not substantive and particular goods.'[1] In the liquidation of religion, which throughout we have seen working in tandem with other cultural forces, political and economic, sexual and ethnocentric, the spirit of God becomes 'the aestheticization of money' and the kingdom of God . . . Las Vegas.[2] 'Religion' becomes a special effect.

The Liquidation of Religion

Religion's white ecstasies lost some of their gothic terror. The abyss came to be encountered more meditatively and the negation of the self and world was conducted more formally. The development of liberal philosophy in the years following the composition of *Moby Dick*, and existential theologies like that of Paul Tillich's, in which religion was orientated towards what was of ultimate concern or the 'depth of reason', facilitated this shift. It was not that the Dionysian had been tamed by the Apollonian. In fact the frenzy and violence of the ultimate reality was perhaps more intense – so intense that representation of it demanded even greater degrees of abstraction. As Nietzsche realized, 'hysteria's smooth surfaces suppress violence'. Controlled surfaces became tense and dramatic with restrained possibilities. The tragic heart of darkness was given a highly organized expression in which mathematics and aesthetics joined forces.

By the late twentieth century we find the French Jesuit and historian Michel de Certeau composing a prose-poem entitled 'White Ecstasy' just months before his death. Luce Giard, the French executor of his literary estate, divined in this writing an encounter between de Certeau and the angel of death. Certainly, the staging of the conversation narrated resembles Antonius Block's game of chess with Death on the beach in Ingmar Bergman's film *The Seventh Seal*. The distance of an allegorical artificiality similarly governs de Certeau's writing. Two men, Simeon the monk and an unnamed visitor from Panoptie, meet on a mountain top to discuss 'the exorbitant goal of the millennial march – many times millennial – of travellers who have set out to see God'. It is Simeon who speaks, not from his own experience but according to those who have written about their experiences of seeing God. Thus, writing screens both of them from the 'dazzling death' that Simeon will describe. For 'the vision coincides with the disappearance of things seen'. 'To see God is, in the end, to see nothing', Simeon explains. In a manner that draws close to Ishmael's narrative, he speaks of such 'seeing' as a 'devouring', a 'blindness', a 'terrifying thing', a 'ship-wreck', and a return to 'the initial "tohu-bohu" that preceded all distinction, according to the first chapter of Genesis'.

> Here is what the final bedazzlement would be: an absorption of objects and subjects in the act of seeing. No violence, only the unfolding of presence. Neither fold nor hole. Nothing hidden and nothing visible. A light without limits, without distance; neuter, in a sense, and continuous. It is only possible to speak of it in relation to our cherished activities, which are utterly annihilated there . . . Our works are gently engulfed in this silent ecstasy, without disaster and without noise, simply having become futile, our world . . . ends.

The apocalyptic is muted, the screaming birds that accompany the engulfment of the *Pequod* are silenced, the violence is more like the clean slice of a razor blade across a volunteered wrist. The Dionysian ecstasy is without struggle or drama. The disappearance draws no attention to itself. The mystic's apprehension of the futility of the world is accompanied by the exhaustion of ennui. Until the final paragraph.

For we recall that Simeon is merely reciting the experiences of others, while the visitor throughout the narration makes no response. But in the final paragraph, the direction of the monologue is dramatically reversed. The visitor from Panoptie, the 'shadowless plain', replies. And in replying he not only affirms Simeon's words, he dissolves the literary distance between narrator and the narrative experiences he has narrated. 'I have known this', he states, simply, adding: 'there is no other end of the world'. And the blank page follows, as if we, like Simeon, now have to encounter the cosmic futility where 'there is no more reading' and 'no more interpretation'. We are all engulfed by the silence of the margins. For this is all there is. This is the ultimate concern, the nothing that subtends the frenetic display of signs and gestures. All 'our cherished activities' are only so many entertaining facades in a 'shadowless plain' – like the fantasy palaces of Las Vegas constructed in the desert.

The French sociologist Jean Baudrillard stated in 1990 that 'If I were asked to characterize the present state of affairs, I would describe it as "after the orgy" . . . Now all we do is simulate the orgy, simulate liberation. We may pretend to carry on in the same direction, accelerating, but in reality we are accelerating in a void, because all the goals of liberation are already behind us.'[3] True religion consumes itself, for it consumes all religious specificities, while meaning itself and value itself become fashion-led and therefore arbitrary. As a concept religion implodes. Having radically dematerialized its institutions and liturgies, sacred texts and solemn rites, confessions and invocations – true religion becomes pantomime (with all the rich etymology of that word); it becomes simulation.

In de Certeau's 'White Ecstasy' the narrator does not return from the silence that engulfs him. He makes no response to the visitor's reply. There is no Ishmael, then, left to tell the story. The 'speak[ing] of it in relation to our cherished activities' has been 'utterly annihilated there'. Art, as religion's supplement, as the formal expression of the sublime experience, also dissolves. It too becomes simulacra; a surface without depth.

The Evacuation of Expression

This implosion of the aesthetic was always a threatened possibility with aesthetics orientated towards the sublime. We can glimpse the near-edge of this implosion in the suburban outskirts of downtown Houston. Among quiet, tree-lined streets and clapboard, gabled houses, stands the Rothko Chapel. Founded by John and Dominique de Menil, and inspired by the abstract expressionism of Mark Rothko's work, the chapel was dedicated in 1971. It is a space for the use of all religions. It is also a space for the housing of fourteen paintings executed by Rothko between 1965 and 1966. Art and religion, gallery and chapel, are extensions of each other. Outside the building, at the centre of a shallow rectangle of water, stands a sculpture by Barnett Newman entitled 'Broken Obelisk'. Here, perched at the apex of a pyramid stands the tip of an obelisk that, like a giant pencil, rises for several metres before abruptly terminating in a jagged edge.

The chapel itself is a low windowless octagon of a pale red brick into which one large double door is set. To some it resembles a mausoleum (it was dedicated almost a year to the day Mark Rothko committed suicide in his New York studio). To others it resembles a womb (the close maternal interior of the chapel being contrasted with Newman's phallic sculpture). To Dominique de Menil, 'Its adoption by Hindus, Jews, Christians and Muslims, by Buddhists and agnostics and by the young in quest of the ultimate, has turned it into a universal sanctuary'. As a sanctuary it forms a retreat not from urban pace and compromise, but from suburban banality and settlement. It is a sanctuary that resembles a bunker. Entering the building, beyond the tourists' foyer, one enters an open space furnished only with benches that can be randomly arranged and re-arranged and two black pillows on the floor. The walls are textured and grey save for where the fourteen large paintings hang. Seven of the paintings are black rectangles with rust-red borders, seven are plum monochromes. The paintings are arranged in three triptychs (two along side walls and one in a recessed apse), four angle-wall paintings and a single painting on the rear wall. Dominique de Menil writes: 'Such monuments, such artists – their toils and hopes, their anguish and victory – have given the Chapel a spiritual aura'. 'Aura', since Walter Benjamin, has sacralized secular aesthetics, as-cribing to the authentic art-piece a 'real presence'. But it is not of presence that this place speaks. It speaks of absence. And de Menil's rhetoric of 'adoption' masks some of the arbitrariness and politics of the founding of this sacred and aesthetic site, and how its sacrality has been subsequently controlled.

For Rothko's chapel was not conceived as 'a universal sanctuary' but a Roman Catholic chapel for the nearby college of St Thomas Aquinas (a Catholic university patronized by the de Menil family). But conflict between priests and patrons resulted in a rethink: 'the site of the still-unbuilt chapel was moved from the campus community . . . and put under the control of Houston's Institute for Religion and Human Development, an ecumenical organization on whose board John de Menil sat'.[4] Religion as human development was the first to 'adopt' the idea of founding a 'universal sanctuary', a spiritual site devoted to that Tillichian phrase 'the ultimate'. As for Rothko himself, throughout the execution of his commission and throughout the help he gave with the design of the building to house it, the prospect of a Catholic context remained. The Christian roots of the project, like the Christian roots of 'religion', surface with the apse at the north end, the triptychs (that traditionally were altar-pieces portraying the crucifixion) and the octagonal design (typical of baptisteries and tombs). And while Christianity is reduced to a few formal gestures that are half-echoes of a tradition under erasure, it was the de Menils who fostered the idea of their ecumenical spirituality.

Rothko produced for them Tillich's 'ultimate'. The large canvases are as uncompromising as they are impenetrable. The maroons are pressed out by the dominance of the flat, black voids, as if the Dionysian moment has always hidden a tragedy of unspeakable despair. While there is a certain play among the forms, their location, and the manner in which the light lifts or pans their colours, and while the tourists who move from one to the other mime this play, there is no drama. There is movement but no room for the spontaneity of drama. What tourists in the visitor's book describe as 'peace' or 'tranquillity' is really the experience of degree zero; it is the numbness, almost the paralysis, of futility. The tourists are zombied; all action takes place in indecision. The dark opacities signal nothing, and they would be nothing – and art itself would end in meaningless daubs – if it were not for how they signal that nullity in calculated and measured ways. So no one can 'Rage, rage against the dying of the light' (Dylan Thomas) in the same way as Ahab or Zarathustra. There is no room for hyperbole, for polemic. There is a complex enervation of such passion in the face of violence so controlled that on the surface what appears is blank indifference. It is this unnerving control that suggests the ritualistic while utterly denying the sacred. It is as if Rothko, the Jew who had lost his faith, was painting the very extremities of a confession that would be housed, he thought, and may be somehow redeemed, in the Roman Catholic context of the mass. The precision of their execution, their arrangement, their composition – these are the only traces of that 'human development' the de Menils worked for. Otherwise, what is encountered in this space is the inhuman; the very opposite of that liberal humanism that championed ecumenical tolerance. Here stands a poignant irony, put succinctly as 'whatever the ecumenical services within, the chapel is about a dark God'.[5] If it is about a God at all.

The leaflet on the chapel available in the foyer sets out its credentials as 'a place of worship receptive to the essence and rites of ceremonies being performed'. There is a dateline of important ecumenical occasions celebrated between March 1978 and October 1996. But the space is convertible, for a list of significant colloquia follows and, besides acting as a small conference centre, the chapel hosts a number of human rights events and presentations. The chapel, then, and Rothko's ironic portrayal of the evacuation of expression, are framed by the glossolalia of a thousand different 'spiritual leaders', the cultural politics of liberal democracy and the economic confidence of Texas oil. The de Menils have actively developed the building as a centre for 'universal friendship' and 'spiritual richness'. The de Menils commissioned the production of important 'spiritual' interpretations of Rothko's work – by Susan J. Barnes and Sheldon Nodelman; they acquired the house and land adjacent to the chapel upon which the Newman sculpture now stands in its reflected pool. In the mid-1980s Dominique de Menil approached the Italian postmodern architect Renzo Piano to design and build a large private museum to house the de Menil collection to the west of the chapel and the Menil Foundation then acquired the surrounding four blocks of the neighbourhood to control the environment. Effectively, as one of Rothko's biographers observes, 'the Rothko Chapel today sits, enclosed, in a kind of town of art'.[6] Rothko's violent nihilism, his struggles with the absurd and the arbitrary that implode the values of both religion and art, have been packaged. On the other side of the liquidation of religion and the evacuation of expression lies the theme park.[7] The final reification of the aesthetic – that the 'town' is on the way to effecting, but doesn't quite – is the kitsch.

The Sublime as Kitsch

Theme parks are highly controlled environments, but the degree of control is rendered invisible so that the circulation of distraction and entertainment and the free flows of cash or credit can proceed as if unbridled. Prometheus unbound has now become desire unlimited. The ultimate experience is measured by the length and perdurance of an adrenalin rush. Self-transcendence is the cost of a ride; and the excellence of the ride is calculated in terms of how close to experiencing raw violence one can come . . . in safety. What matters is encountering the extreme; what lures is the limit. The transcendence of the self has become the transportation of the self, at the highest speeds possible, approximating the instantaneous. Transcendence is equated with experiencing intensity or extremity.

A culture that focuses upon the spectacular and attempts to produce endless intensities and excitements might be termed, then, a transcendental culture. Later we will have to ask what kind of transcendence this is. For the moment it is evident that in such a culture religion will come to matter, not as private consolation or subjective rapture, but as public resource. What kind of resource we will also have to return to, but in being made a public resource 'religion' is again transformed. The disciplining of the self which became the negation of the self has now become the dematerialization of the self in a fantasy reflected in and modelled on *Star Trek*'s most famous line: 'beam me up Scottie'. The sublime itself has been sublated, and we have arrived at the extremities of the superficial (that are packaged as profundities). Consummation (the prolongation of the orgasmic height or what the postmodern philosophers of desire call *jouissance*) is now ostentatiously allied with consumerism. But the demand is the same: the fully immersive experience.

'It is a total sensory experience', explains Bill Coan, 'that is educational, historical, theatrical, and evangelistic – blending sights, sounds and tastes that transport guests 7,000 miles away and 3,000 years back in time.' The advertising puffery explains:

When guests enter The Holy Land Experience from the parking area through the Jerusalem City Gate they immediately leave the 20th century behind and find themselves totally immersed

121

in a thriving, colorful, and fascinating first-century AD street market. The authenticity is enhanced with Middle Eastern music, village craftsmen, themed shops – including The Old Scroll Shop, which offers a large selection of genuine biblical artefacts, Bibles, books, and gifts – and costumed dramatists, punctuated with taped background sounds.

Bill Coan is principal of Orlando-based ITEC Entertainment Corporation. Founded in 1985, ITEC specializes in creating immersive experiences through advanced technological special effects. It has designed sites for Sea World, NASA/Kennedy Space Center, Blockbuster Entertainment, Walt Disney and Universal Studios. The Holy Land Experience is a Bible-based theme park situated in Orlando between Disneyland (Florida) and Universal Studios. It is one of two such theme parks in the States. The other is a more low-key, country-walk affair called Holy Land, USA, in Virginia. Money is being raised (the minimum contribution is $10,000) for a more interactive site in Pennsylvania that boasts the possibility of experiencing a raging tempest on the Sea of Galilee in a 'pendulum boat' that will swing out over a shallow indoor lake in a geodesic dome.

> As the boat swings higher and higher, the attraction will simulate the pitching and tossing of a boat in a storm at sea. There will be wind, thunder, lightning, and wind-driven spray. The ride may be wet and guests will be offered the loan of slickers. At the apex of the ride, an actor portraying Jesus will stand up in the middle of the boat and calm the raging tempest. See Mark 4: 39. Background music will feature Jessy Dixon and the Gather Homecoming Choir singing *Master, the Tempest Is Raging*.[8]

We need to examine in more detail the nature of the immersion that is being offered here. Primarily it is sensuous: the food, the smells, the sounds, the sights, the feelings of a recreated religious past. 'Research', 'knowledge' and 'education' are high-cultural dressing for sound-bite information that is secondary to the experience. The extent to which the experience is immersive will depend upon the effective organization of the various images (visual, auditory, tactile, olfactory and gustatory) to solicit the desires and expectations of the 'visitors'. An investment must be made (financial and existential), and a surrender to the bombardment of the senses by signs which reproduce not the true artefacts, but the concatenation of fantasies and interpretations of what has come to constitute *for us Westerners* the 'Holy Land'. The simulations are to be enjoyed *as* simulations, the surface *as* surface.

These immersive, interactive and simulated environments signify the collapse of the sublime into the kitsch. They point to the other side of Rothko's burden of the void – when the surface is just surface, when the art of the nothing becomes the irrelevance of or the indifference to the aesthetic. Classical aesthetics (which has been just two centuries in the making) has always wished to separate the sublime from the kitsch – though both are indebted to the excesses (mystical and material) of the baroque. The sublime, as we saw in chapter 3, was related to the infinite and the most profound, the ultimate and the unpresentable. The kitsch, on the other hand, is unrepentant about its superficiality and its artificiality. The kitsch is self-consciously theatrical and flaunts its ephemerality. The kitsch announces a certain bankruptcy of meaning in clever, ironic ways. It trades in experiences of the profound that are either deflated or over-inflated; transcendence is engineered. What is aimed at is awe in the face of the spectacular; wonder achieved through special effects. These experiences of awe and wonder are as evanescent as they are instantaneous; they are convenient and easy satisfactions. They have to be seized while the opportunity is there. While they are in town they are 'unmissable'. As such, the kitsch is inseparable from the commodification of time; time as a series of instants whose value is calculated, whose contents must be sucked dry. The kitsch is unashamed commodification, reification, idolatry; a combination of the fabulous, the seductive and the fetishized. It generates fantasies while glorying in aesthetic inadequacy; in art's failure to express. It erases the boundary between high art and popular culture, placing importance on look, style, presentation and performance. And these are all, in the educational jargon, 'transferable skills', not simply located in the cabaret but practised in everyday life, bought and sold on the high street. Cultivating the look, the image, creating the lifestyle, are postmodern preoccupations with the aesthetics of the

123

everyday. Freedom is experienced as the consumer's ability to chose between the varieties of fantasies, escapes, and transportations on offer. Like surfing the net, the adrenalin pumps as the resources for pleasure, information (infotainment) and diversion are drained from one site before passing to another. The Romantic's infinite desire has become consumer greed. Cinema and television have been at the forefront of providing fantasies for the masses, but with theme parks, shopping malls as theme parks, themed pubs, interactive museums, heritage trails, expo exhibitions, hotels and cybergames these fantasies are now three dimensional and constitute the very fabric of our urban and domestic environments. The fantasies are continually being inhabited. We are immersed within them such that one moves from one fetishized location to another. The Holy Land experiences are fetishisms of faith.

While each of these projects state loudly that they are 'non-profit making organizations', what with charges for the rides, the 'themed shops', the sale of 'genuine biblical artefacts, Bibles, books, and gifts' and restaurants and cafés (hawking 'Goliath-burgers' and 'Camel-coolers'), infotainment does not come cheap. The Holy Land Experience cost $16 million to create and took ten years to realize (opening in February 2001). That investment will be recouped in some way. But besides the link between religion and capitalism (which is now explicit), what is of further interest about these projects, and significant for this argument, is who the project is financed by and designed to cater for. The Holy Land Experience is aimed at both Jewish and Christian customers. Its emphasis is upon the Bible as history and while it officially hopes 'Christians can come to be encouraged and reinforced in their faith', the project is the dream-child of 'Zion Hopes', an organization headed up by Marvin Rosenthal (a Jewish convert to Christianity?). Considerable emphasis is given in the theme park to ancient Jewish history and religious practices. The Holy Lands of Pennsylvania and Virginia are aimed at America's conservative evangelicals. What each project demonstrates is that with the liquidation of religion and the evacuation of expression has also come the return to committed faith-based practices and tradition-based reasoning (which liberalism can only mark in terms of right-wing politics and religious fundamentalism). We will return to this later. For the moment, we must recognize the complex combination of experience-hungry consumerism and religious simulation. We saw the religious experience as a consuming one and how this related to the figure of the cannibal as the feared and awed consumer. Now, in the West at least, we can recognize how the logic of that association has developed. The religious experience is inseparable from a consumer experience. The consumer experience (consumer therapy) and the religious experience are both desire-driven and aim at immediate satisfaction. The Slovenian cultural theorist Slavoj Žižek observes with respect to 'Western' Buddhism and Taoism as the spiritual ideologies of global capitalism:

> instead of trying to cope with the accelerating rhythm of technological progress and social changes, one should rather renounce the very endeavour to retain control over what goes on, rejecting it as the expression of the modern logic of domination – one should, instead, 'let oneself go', drift along, while retaining an inner distance and indifference towards the mad dance of this accelerated process . . . If Max Weber were alive today, he would definitely write a second, supplementary, volume to his *Protestant Ethic*, entitled *The Taoist Ethic and the Spirit of Global Capitalism*.

As such religions become fetishized, they provide commodities that 'enable[s] you to fully participate in the frantic pace of the capitalist game while sustaining the perception you are not really in it'.[9] After the void, then, religion is a matter of simulations; the simulation of a special effect. We encountered this combination of religion and consumer excess in Luhrmann's *Romeo & Juliet*. They are signs of a postsecular culture.

Postsecular Culture

As I said in chapter 1, what is understood as religious is related to what is understood by the secular. The sacred establishes itself with respect to the profane, the supernatural to the natural. The progress of the secular from *Moby Dick* to the present day can be measured in church attendance (for Christians) and the changing habits of each generation. Any secularization process is complex and particular to political and national circumstances. In its early stages it combined anti-clericalism and sceptical reasoning with the autonomous power of the state to legislate on behalf of its citizens. It opened a sphere in which religious tolerance was made possible by segregating private convictions from public office. Capitalism could flourish independent of ecclesial check and censure. Nineteenth-century liberalism defined the political aims and the anthropological orientation of secularization. Hence John Henry Newman, among several other Christians of a conservative persuasion, regarded 'the spirit of liberalism as the characteristic of the destined Antichrist'. Of course liberalism developed out of the translation of Christian teaching into a universal, moral and natural religion – as its dedication to the defence and expansion of human rights and the freedom of conscience makes evident. The liberal democratic claim – still sounded by advocates of globalism, like Fukuyama – that 'liberal democracy is the final form of human government' and therefore the only legitimate form of social order – is a demythologized account of all religions leading to Christianity as the consummate religion. Demythologization was the intellectual process of secularization just as what Weber termed *Entzauberung* or disenchantment was the technological process of secularization. Liberalism fostered both processes that it might bring about social salvation and redemption from those forces repressing human freedom through secular means, through the institutions of the necessarily secular state. Secularity as such came to be associated with 'impartiality'; as not itself an ideology but the unbiased judge of all ideologies. In fact, liberalism became the beneficent unmasker of all ideologies and demagogues. Allied with an ever-increasing confidence in scientific reasoning, it 'exposed' all forms of superstition, challenged all ignorances and set in process a radical demystification of the world. As a political philosophy it demanded the free flows of democratic debate and the minimum of state intervention in such flows. As an economic philosophy of *laissez-faire* it established the market-place and market-forces as prime determining factors in the distribution and accumulation of wealth. As a social and cultural philosophy what began as religious tolerance must culminate in tolerance *tout court* – human rights meant rights for women, rights of gays and lesbians, rights for animals, rights against coercion, the right to be respected whatever one's ethnic origins. As the historian Owen Chadwick put it in his 1973–4 Gifford Lectures: 'From the moment that European opinion decided for toleration, it decided for an eventual free market in opinion'.[10] Liberalism fostered a hegemonic moral code understood as universal, egalitarian and progressive which defined the character, as well as demanding the existence of, secularity.

But contained within the cultural logic of liberalism, and therefore secularity, was its own demise. It negotiated pluralism and difference on the basis of an essential, metaphysical unity: the value of human life. Such humanism was far too frail a foundation. Death camps, genocides and world wars questioned optimistic accounts of being human, while liberalism's commitment to individual rights fostered an increasing social atomism. As the boundaries of the liberal state were being compromised externally by world-systems of trade and finance, public consensus was being compromised internally by the clash of incommensurate values. While postmodern philosophers radicalized difference and extolled the other in the name of the wholly other (often co-opting religious language to do so), global economics was forcing labour to become increasingly mobile and civil warfare conducted with international financing was creating shifting populations of refugees. The Western nation-states and North America were called culturally to respect difference *as* difference while increasingly having to take what had been a hitherto right-wing stance with respect to their immigration policies. The state, which had become the guarantor of impartial, even-handed justice, was increasingly criticized for its structural blindnesses: that it was the purveyor of white, male, middle-class and heterosexual ideologies. The state was seen as founded upon the exclusion and violation of others. The processes by which it disciplined its population, the processes by which certain norms of behaviour and expectation were naturalized, were being called into question and resisted. Differences were insisted upon, inequalities were named, as multiple forms of reason, standpoints, traditions and perspectives demanded their right to flourish.

It is not simply that the axioms of liberalism – universalism, egalitarianism, belief in progress towards a better social life – crumbled. In fact, as I have pointed out, certain spin doctors of globalism are reformulating these axioms on the basis of expanding free-market capitalism. But these axioms of liberalism are only one option now in the vast trading of opinion and belief. As Jean-François Lyotard argues in his influential book *The Postmodern Condition*, the grand explanatory narratives, of which liberalism was one (and Marxism and scientific positivism others), have now become *petits récits* – one of the possible ways of giving an account of the world. In the postmodern world, secular reasoning too becomes just another narrative (*récit*).

Around the helter-skelter towards the cultural relativisms and the syncretisms emerging from these overlapping, cited and recited narratives, a sceptical question (raised after the Paris riots of May 1968 by Michel de Certeau) continually circulates: what makes a belief believable? Why accept one story rather than another? That is, in the plethora of viewpoint and interpretation, attention is repeatedly drawn to the persuasive rhetorics in which opinion is couched and canvassed. Attention is drawn to the circulation of signs and the suspicion of their vacuity. So that it is not just that there are no intrinsic values commonly identifiable (and uncontestable), but that in the multitude of contending values each of these values is part of a persuasive package. Values are inseparable from lifestyles and all lifestyles today are designed, marketed and sold to us. Of course the illusion is maintained that each of us chooses and as such the preferences of the individual confer value. But in a semiotically driven – that is a media-driven – culture preferences are guided, informed, shaped and constructed. The illusions of choice are maintained in what Adorno called 'the liquidation of the individual'.

When the foundations and essentialisms of liberalism collapse, when liberalism comes to recognize that despite its appeal to the ground of nature it was a construction (as was its understanding of nature), then the 'howling infinite' upon which the flows of public opinion sail makes absence palpable. That does not mean that liberalism is dead. Far from it. The traditions of liberal thinking remain, provoking as well as trying to resolve culture wars, as we shall see. But the foundations having subsided, the structures built upon those foundations will subsequently turn into mortared shells. Increasingly, the secular world produced and policed by liberalism becomes a necessary fiction. The secular worldview implodes because it realizes

(Hegel would say consummates) the logic of its own destiny: it is a virtual reality.[11]

There are two effects of postsecularism that are significant for understanding the character of religion in postmodernity. The first concerns the reversal of Weber's 'disenchantment-by-technological-advancement' thesis, and the second concerns the re-entrenchment of theological traditions.

Re-enchantment

Ironically, the technology that Weber observed controlling and calibrating the world is the means by which that same world has been re-enchanted. Rather than scientific reasoning and instrumental thinking leading to reductive, positivist and behaviourist accounts of the way things are, such reasoning and thinking has promoted itself through emphasizing its inventive power, its creativity, its imaginative scope. Allied with the glitter of the media and advanced telecommunications, technology has become sexy, seductive and the bearer of messianic possibilities. As Jacques Derrida in an important essay entitled 'Faith and Knowledge' observes, 'because one increasingly *uses* artefacts and prostheses of which one is totally ignorant, in a growing disproportion between knowledge and know-how, the space of such technical experience tends to become more animistic, magical, mystical'.[12] The important verb here, italicized by Derrida, is 'use'. Science is no longer just out there providing tools for mastering the planet and for domestic convenience; it is creating the milieux in which we live. We *use* it as we continually *interact* with it. In fact, given the high number of micro-processors in the average Western household (over 100) and the desire to get them increasingly to speak with each other and create integrated, intelligent environments, the technology has moved beyond the prosthetic. The immersive experiences of an aestheticized life are made possible and maintained by advanced technology. If anything is prosthetic today, it is the human body itself. Hence, talk about 'digital living' becomes heady with the possibilities for 'techno-transcendence' and the language of light offers undreamt of freedoms.

129

But the re-enchantment – though effected and disseminated by contemporary technological breakthroughs, particularly in telecommunications – goes beyond the technological. Since the 'slasher' movies of the 1970s there has been a cultural reaffirmation of the gothic expressing itself on a number of social levels: the 'goth' look; the mass international consumption of the Harry Potter series; the fascination with the psychopath; and the lurid worlds of cybergames like *Doom*, *Crypt*, *Diablo* and *Warrior Kings*. The gothic reintroduces Gnosticism into the cultural imagination: dark forces battle in apocalyptic fashion with the powers of light. There is the fashion for angels, on the one hand, and fascination with vampires, the demonic and the undead, on the other. And whereas evil in modernity was understood as social and anthropological (corruption, violence, tyranny being exercised by human beings), evil in postmodernity is concerned with the unknown and the indeterminate; forces that render human defences inadequate. This differs from Romantic gothic not in its sensationalism and its desire to exploit and stimulate fear, but in its eclecticism. For as numerous novels, computer games, films and television programmes testify the gothic host now includes alien predators, cyborgs, androids and intergalactic imperial warfare, on the one hand, and prehistoric carnivores on the other. A recent sociological analysis of this material concludes: 'If I were pressed to submit one reason for the contemporary proliferation of the Gothic, that reason would in a certain sense be religious . . . With the contemporary turn to the Gothic . . . we recover a horizon of ultimate meaning. We recover something of what is lost with the withdrawal of God from the day to day world.'[13] We can note the vagueness of 'in a certain sense' and the appeal to the 'ultimate' that is focused on absence or 'the withdrawal of God'. We can observe that contemporary religion is not about God, but the absence of God.

The production sites of this new techno-gothic lie not just in the visual media. The eminent French historian of science Michel Serres published in 1993 a book entitled (in English) *Angels: A Modern Myth*, in which he argues for a parallelism between angelic messengers and electric communication. The parallelism is used to suggest that we live in a world in which there are constant flows of information between the animate and the inanimate, the technological

130

and the divine. Luce Irigaray, the Belgian feminist and philosopher, also speaks of angels, Christ and the trinity in order to outline the permeability of the sexuate body and the need to develop gender-conscious accounts of becoming divine. Slavoj Žižek has recently turned his attention to evil and the haunting, abyssal absence at the root of human psyche, the Real. Jean Baudrillard and Jacques Derrida have similarly been drawn to discussing radical evil. There is a production of the religious, then, in academic conversation that is also re-enchanting our understanding of the world.

This new cultural imaginary enters the everyday, if not the banal, in the urban landscape itself. And its positioning with respect to the more traditional forms of religious observation is apposite. Manchester is a thriving post-industrial city in the north of England, probably second only to London in the British Isles for its wealth creation, population and contribution to gross national product. The city centre has, over recent years, been completely revamped, partly with a view to making a bid to stage the Olympic Games and because it will host the Commonwealth Games in the summer of 2002, partly with a view to luring major international companies into the area through its image as a global city. In the revamping the traditional churches have been marginalized. A Unitarian Chapel can be found in the heart of the financial district, but from the outside it resembles one more bank. A beautiful Anglo-Catholic church known locally as the Hidden Gem is down a side street off a square that is the urban and suburban focus for civic administration. There is Manchester Cathedral, but it lies outside the public space marked by the shopping malls, a major entertainment centre, an 'authentic' Tudor pub and the Museum of the Modern City. A number of city churches just outside the main thoroughfares have become discount warehouses and storage companies. Nevertheless, there is a public presence of religion. Over a barber's and body piercer's shop-front is the name 'Parting the Waves'. By the name stands a large painted figure of a very muscular-looking Jesus (who ought to be Moses) in a pair of shades. There is a well-known vegetarian café and shop under the sign 'The Eighth Day'. Few will get the subtleties of this phrase, though the owners seem to know it provenance. The eighth day is usually celebrated in the Christian liturgical calendar on 1 January (or the Feast of the Circumcision). The eighth day

131

signifies the day following the Sabbath rest, that is, the eschatological day of resurrection when not only the bodies but also the souls of those who have died in faith will be brought to new life. The shop, besides selling various organic foodstuffs available in the café, functions as a New Age warehouse, with stocks of scented candles, sticks of incense, crystal mobiles, and all the arcana of aromatherapy, astrology and white witchcraft. A sandwich shop sports the trade name 'Feed the 5 Thousand' and an employment bureau calls itself 'Angels'. In the famous clubbing district, there are venues called 'Babylon', 'Paradise Factory' and 'The Font'. The latter welcomes and solicits its clientele with the words 'be baptised'.

The liquidation of religion evidently does not mean its end. Too many have pronounced the end of 'religion' prematurely – like Karl Barth (in the 1920s) and Wilfred Cantwell Smith (in the 1950s). The liquidation of religion is accomplished in its increasing dilution. The resources of faith traditions – historical, symbolic, liturgical, textual, mythic – are being endlessly redeployed, reiterated and dispersed beyond the communities for whom they have a specific content and significance. This has always happened. Syncretism is nothing new; it is the foundational process of cultural transformation. Hellenism was absorbed by Judaism, Judaism was in cultural negotiation with the Romans and the Christians, and had developed its own sects like the Essenes. More recently Hinduism and Buddhism have been filtered through Orientalism into Western thinking. No one can police the boundaries of a discursive practice, despite repeated attempts to draw the lines between orthodoxy and heresy by torture and coercion of the unconverted, excommunication or the slaying of the 'infidel'. But what is different today is the extent of the reiteration and dispersal. This goes not only for 'religion'. It is seen with productions of the aesthetic and the political. All three domains were one-time sites of moral value. But moral value has increasingly been conflated with the exchange value of goods, the sign value of brand names and advertising. 'Religion' is lending a certain magical, mystical polish to contemporary forms of customized transcendence. Having come to define itself in terms of the ultimate and the void, the absence and the withdrawal of God, religion enters its own kenosis and empties itself of intrinsic value and significance. Religion does not live in and of itself any more – it lives in commercial business, gothic and sci-fi fantasy, in health clubs, themed bars and architectural design, among happy-hour drinkers, tattooists, ecologists and cyberpunks. Religion has become a special effect, inseparably bound to an entertainment value. It plays two mutually implicated roles in contemporary Western culture. On the one hand, as symbolic capital with a certain charismatic past, it can give places, goods, even people, a mystic charge. Those allured by this charge are not buying religion, they are not consuming the religious or being consumed by it; they are consuming the illusions or simulations of religion. On the other hand, these simulations of religion, religion as symbolic capital, are used as an aesthetic diversion from the profound uncertainties, insecurities and indeterminacies of postmodern living. The religious is used rhetorically in the creation of the illusions of transcendence, to help simulate euphoria in transporting events. Both cultural roles are different aspects of religion as fetish – caught up in the complex economies of displaced desire (sexual and consumerist); desire without a proper object. Where religious traditions and practices retain a strong sense of identity and remain substantial, they are, as Manuel Castells terms it, 'resistant identities'. In a culture of intensities and extremities, confessional communities produce their own fetishisms of faith.

Confessionalism

In chapter 3 I pointed to a certain resistance to 'religion' voiced by Schleiermacher and the development from 'positive religion' to 'theology'. Theology is concerned with articulating the theo-logic of a faith – a reasoning that takes place on the basis of an acceptance of the doctrines and the disciplines of a believing community. These communities operated before and during the various transformations in 'religion'. The word 'theology' has, like 'religion', an extensive and colourful past. The early Christian church rejected it as a descriptive category because its provenance was ancient Greek paganism. It was current throughout the medieval church as a synonym for 'the Faith'. Schleiermacher readopted it, but until recently the word 'theology' was understood as only applicable to Christianity. Now a number of other faiths (Judaism, Islam and Hinduism, notably) speak of their theologies.

The term 'theology' is often used reactively. The people using it either reject the kind of descriptions of beliefs and their practice made by specialists in 'the study of religion', or do not identify with the vacuous 'spirituality' that we have seen is often understood as the essence of religion. In the 1920s, in the second edition of his *Letter to the Romans*, Karl Barth fulminated against the empty notions of 'religion'. For Barth, 'religion' could only trade in emptinesses because it lacked the true content of God's revelation in Christ. It trafficked in unbelief or pseudo-believing because it was merely a projection of human desire, 'the Godless human being'. Christianity was 'the true religion'. Since the early 1980s there has been a noticeable turn to 'theology'; to arguing and acting from an explicit confessional standpoint. Sociologists have related this trend to the international changes in trade that followed the oil crisis, the termination of the GATT (General Agreement on Tariffs and Trade) agreement, the detachment, by America, from the gold standard, and the pressures to modernize or go into terminal decline. The same economic influences, then, that are seen as significant for the advent of postmodernity and the development of globalism, are held responsible for the increased popularity of belonging to a confessing community. In an 'increasingly globalized world – characterized by historically exceptional degrees of civilizational, societal and other modes of interdependence and widespread consciousness thereof – there is an *exacerbation* of civilizational, societal and ethnic self-consciousness', a concomitant of which is 'the return to the sacred'.[14] The resurgence of religion in the last decades of the twentieth century – which shows no sign of abating – is most striking in the missionizing religions. Christianity and Islam are expanding, particularly in Africa and, for Christianity, South Korea. These communities, or revivalist groups, are as diverse as evangelical Christianity, Islamic 'fundamentalism', conservative Roman Catholicism, Neo-Barthianism and Hasidic Judaism. They are not all extremist. Many embrace a broad-based traditionalism. But a new Reformation is emerging in which these communities constitute themselves as 'resistance identities' in a world that has become radically different from, and threatening to the existence of, the truth-claims for which they stand. In the face of cultural divergence and secular materialism there is adaptation or separatism, syncretism or purism, negotiation or war.

Throughout history there have always been faith communities who proclaimed that they stood for the true form of the faith. If there is anything new about the contemporary forms of theological conservatism, it is their public assertiveness. In the West, with the promulgation of religious toleration and the rise of modern 'religion', a politics of politeness effectively managed 'enthusiasms' – though there have been forms of national identity that have not only persecuted but also 'cleansed' the state of religious minorities associated with alien ethnicities. But the various forms of Christian fundamentalism, evangelical revivals and neo-orthodoxies have been accommodated within the existing structures of liberal government in the West – even if only by ghettoizing them. Where that accommodation has been impossible (as in the conflict between Protestants and Catholics in Northern Ireland), again more is at stake than the differences between two Christian cultures – there is a whole history of national and civic identity.

The theologically conservative aggression in the face of a politics of politeness has to be situated within wider cultural trends in postmodernity, particularly globalization, the confidence given to minority groups as both a result of liberalism and the critiques it has fostered (postcolonialism, for example), a general nostalgia for and a commodification of the historical, and the rise of neo-tribalism. We might put this more briefly: the politics of politeness has been transplanted by a politics of difference. The developing sense of the erosion of local, national and religious characteristics, in the advance of a monoculture fostered by an international trade dominated by Western lifestyles, has brought about a return to or reinvestment in the traditional. Since the transformation of cultures is so profoundly caught up in the technological exchange of goods (commodities, information as a commodity, images), then the character of indigenous cultures, their traditional associations and identification, must necessarily change. Globalism, like the computer, is not intrinsically ethical. Its secularism can then radically challenge traditional moral options. Since faith communities are one of the primary maintainers and developers of tradition, resistance to the dissolution of a particular

135

cultural identity finds in them profound resources. The resources of devout practices counter the dissemination of secularized ways of thinking and acting, their advocacy of a brash materialism. This counter-move can be made more aggressive by the sense that societies are pressurized into being part of the global system; by the sense that separation from the flows of capital and worldwide investment would be national suicide. Resistance to change can become heroic, and the enemy – capitalism or secularism – mythological in stature. The rate of this change can be so rapid that countries can implode under the pressure to modernize. Some have argued that this implosion was one of the reasons for the rise of Islamic fundamentalism in post-1979 Iran. As such, a strong resistance identity is formed on the basis of a religious practice and divine laws in order to counter the incursions of capitalism, modernity and secularism. Globalism offers an international identity at odds with, in this case, the Muslim sense of its own collective identity. As article ten of the Iranian constitution states: 'All Muslims form a single nation'.

In the West, Christian fundamentalists are pragmatically much more at home with advanced telecommunications, the media and accumulative capitalism. They have a history of accommodations, although the liberal attitude towards the status of women, gays and lesbians has increasingly caused them to define themselves, and their distinctive positions, more aggressively. Once so defined they engage in what we can term (after James Davison Hunter) 'culture wars' rather than the clash of civilizations (after Samuel Huntington). For these fundamentalists, civil and human rights now become irreconcilable with Bible-based or doctrine-based convictions.

While liberalism facilitated some security from persecution for dissidents and minorities, it also reinforced the identification of the dissident as a member of a minority group and as a potential (or a past) victim. Human rights have been criticized for their negative view of people as victims or potential victims. The effect of identity politics, which flourished in the 1970s, was to build confidence among immigrant communities in their right to assert their own religious traditions and rise above victimage. Alongside this there arose a level of critical reflection in geography, ethnography and anthropology concerning the construction of beliefs and practices of others by first-world thinking. In particular, there was an increasing sensitivity to the way Christian Europe had created the Eastern religions in its own image. The very translation of Eastern sacred texts, and the transcription of rites and devotions, into elite, intellectual and powerful Western languages, was recognized as acts of appropriation. The critical attention to what Edward Said termed 'Orientalism' means that we now wish to hear the subaltern voice, or what those who had been colonized said of themselves and their beliefs. At the same time, this critical attention examined how liberalism itself constructed the other as intransigent (rather than tolerant) and fanatical (rather than responsible citizen). The anthropologist Talal Asad and the sociologist Akbar Ahmed have both pointed to a construction by the West of the Muslim and Arab world and the creation of a moral geography whereby the West represented the free and civilized world.

By the late 1980s and early 1990s the British sociologist Zygmunt Bauman and the French social anthropologist Michel Maffesoli were observing a shift away from society to sociality. The implications of this shift are profound: nothing less than the potential demise of society as the social collapses into the cultural, and the cultural determines the forms and character of relations between individuals. Possessing now no common traditions, in a situation where values are indissociable from lifestyles, then Bauman and Maffesoli suggest we have moved beyond what Benedict Anderson called 'imaginary communities' (such as the nation-state) into a developing neo-tribalism. Neo-tribal forms of relation establish self-consciously defined groupings which, while expressing something of the liberal right to free association, generate a strong sense of belonging that takes priority over any larger civic or national incorporation. These communes share sets of identifications and values that separate them from those who are outside, defining them as distinctive. They are not forms of society associated with particular location, rooted in a history and a tradition, acknowledging consensus on fundamental issues. They are forms of sociality that go in and out of fashion, as the times demand. If a culture is understood as a common way of life, then with neo-tribalism we now have to speak of cultures as self-regarding entities. The current fashion in certain Christian groupings for publishing a catechism that defines who is in and who is out, or statements of faith and mission to which those joining are expected to subscribe, testifies to these forms of identity-building. Within the groups themselves there is a commitment to patriarchal authority and value is made of submission to the law of God. A new politics and policing of theological difference is evident and widespread.

So we have, on the one hand, a re-enchantment of the world in which religion provides a symbolic capital, empty of content and yet preeminently consumable – like caffeine-free, sugar-free Coke. On the other, we have strong theological commitments increasingly confident about voicing, and voicing aggressively, their moral and spiritual difference. Secularism is imploding, liberalism is at an end, and media-driven market values have become lifestyles – so much interior décor and designer diets. A moral and political vacuum opens, which religion (having arrived at a celebration of the void) can do nothing to transcend. In fact, transcendence itself is produced in any number of guises, and it fits remarkably well, as Žižek points out, with a rapacious appetite for the world's goods. So what then of the pursuit of the true religion?

Culture Wars

As the advert states: 'The future is already here'. The politics of difference, which is also a politics of rhetoric – for it is driven by positions being unambivalently and forcefully represented – is bound to lead to culture wars.[15] But in these wars there is a sense in which where we are in the West today is a transitional stage. While a tradition of liberal, secular humanist thinking survives there will be struggles to rescue the liberal project as a political philosophy. Though national boundaries are increasingly transgressed by international finance and trading, democracy will be rethought – perhaps in larger geographical units. This rescue will not extend to liberalism as a religious project – there is not the same pragmatic need. Only academics will play around with so-called 'secular theologies', religions of the void mixed in with an atheology of the sublime. They will draw students because of their religious interpretations of postmodern philosophers like Levinas and Derrida, rather than because they have anything further to add to the adoration of the *nihil.* For the time being, the search for the true religion is over. Over for two reasons: first, because postmodernity does not trade in truth, it trades in interpretations and informations; second, because where truth remains important it is part of the search for the true faith or being true to the faith – whether that faith is Judaism or Christianity, Hinduism or Islam. And in this call to being faithful to the tradition it does not often establish itself as the enemy of other traditions. For what is remarkable about where we stand today is that various radicalized or conservative theologies – in Judaism, Christianity, Islam and Hinduism – are, in the West, co-existing relatively peacefully, each proclaiming their faith as true. In some case these orthodoxies are forming alliances to lobby against changes in social policy – in education, on issues of human sexuality, on the right to abortion, for example – that seem to them morally wrong. And if they do denounce each other as misguided, they are not raising pogroms and crusades against each other. At the moment we are not returning, then, to the Wars of Religion. Given the vapid meaning 'religion' has today, it is difficult to see how wars could be waged in its name. Each orthodoxy can operate in the same civic space. For the common enemy, at this time, is the ideology of liberalism itself, its self-righteous religious veneer, and the collapse of moral order brought about by an aggressive consumerism that delights in transgressing boundaries.

In Britain this came into sharp focus in the media-hyped responses to the public burning by a group of local Muslims of Salman Rushdie's novel *Satanic Verses*. The event took place on a gloomy Saturday afternoon in Bradford city centre, on 4 January 1989. The burning was ritualized. The protest was organized. Several prominent city people had been invited, including a number of Labour councillors and MPs. It was not then, prime facie, an act of civil disobedience. A wider public attention was sought since the event took place twenty minutes earlier than scheduled because the photographer–journalist from the local newspaper, the *Telegraph and Argus*, had to be elsewhere in Bradford later that afternoon. What is significant is the way this local event among Muslims in Yorkshire first took on national and then international significance. For there had been a similar event staged in Bolton earlier that month which did not receive any attention at all; later, in July of the same year,

139

a fire-bomb attack on a London bookstore, thought at the time to be the responsibility of Muslims protesting against the publication of Rushdie's book, did not engender the same mythologizing. On 17 January Rushdie himself went public on the Bradford event, calling for the condemnation by the Labour Party of those official members who had witnessed the book burning. But the response in Bradford was muted. Only the Labour MP for Bradford South publicly condemned the event; the rest appear to have been dumbfounded by the publicity the book burning had received. Surely this was one more public demonstration, in line with other demonstrations like the anti-Cruise missile and the anti-apartheid campaigns. In the mid-1970s evangelical Christians had vigorously protested outside cinemas showing *The Exorcist*, calling for its censorship. Demonstrations, in a democracy, are surely the very expression of the freedoms the liberal state was there to uphold? Furthermore, the book had been banned in a number of Islamic countries and the British Muslims were seeking to take legal action against Penguin Books under the blasphemy laws. Protests in Pakistan had been far more vociferous.

The Bradford book burning touched a raw national nerve. The posters proclaiming 'Rushdie Must Be Destroyed' introduced a violent and seemingly personal hatred into a public space. The liberal boundary between private and public opinion had been transgressed. There were Leader comments in the country's newspapers, televised interviews, debates and discussions, radio phone-ins. By the end of January 1989 the book burning had become a symbol of a culture war that the British had, until then, been oblivious to. In the months that followed, a term new to British public discourse was officially sanctioned: Islamic fundamentalism. It was a term that gained gravitas when, exactly one month after the event in Bradford, on 4 February 1989, Ayatollah Ruhollah Khomeini issued his fatwa: 'I inform the proud Muslim people of the world that the author of the *Satanic Verses* book which is against Islam, the Prophet and the Koran, and all involved in its publication who were aware of its content, are sentenced to death'. It was a term given more credence in the West with the commencement of the Gulf War two years later.

The nature of this British culture war is significant and illustrative of 'religion' in postmodernity. On the one hand, there is the novel itself and, on the other, the response and awakening it aroused. For in the novel's magic realism the line between the sublime and the kitsch is erased and the world is re-enchanted. The lives of Saladin Chamcha, the actor, and Gibreel Farishta, the movie star, become woven into an account of dreams and visions, angels, prophets and reincarnation. In the late twentieth century these two unbelievers, whose 'long-standing rejecting of the Eternal was beginning to look pretty foolish', reperform the founding stories of the Koran. The novel emphasizes – even while satirizing – the practising of a faith and the thinking that issues from belonging to a tradition. Islam is presented as an embodied commitment, rooted in liturgies, dietary disciplines, the reading and interpretation of sacred books, prayers. In a rich passage Gibreel, ironically reciting a leaflet written by a fundamentalist Christian, ridicules the anonymity of contemporary demythologized 'religion':

> The leaflet argued that even scientists were busily reinventing God, that once they had proved the existence of a single unified force of which electromagnetism, gravity and the strong and weak forces of the new physics were all merely aspects, avatars, one might say, or angels, then what would we have but the oldest thing of all, a supreme entity controlling all creation . . . 'You see, what our friend says is, if you have to choose between some type of disembodied force-field and the actual living God, which one would you go for? Good point, na? You can't pray to an electric current. No point asking a wave-form for the key to Paradise.'

Gibreel adds: 'All bloody bunk . . . Makes me sick', for like Chamcha he effects an atheism that is about to be exploded as the tradition dramatically reinserts itself into their lives. We will come across this irruption of the tradition from within the secular worldview again: it is at the very core of the culture wars I am describing. *Satanic Verses*, then, both represents and develops a postsecular and a post-liberal culture.

It is ironic therefore that the book made manifest a war between liberal and theological values in British society; that the book triggered an irruption of the traditional. It could do this because of its own status as 'literature'. As Talal Asad points out, *Satanic Verses* was not 'just any printed communication' but a novel by a world-renowned writer – even a potential Nobel Prize winner. The book's contents were postliberal and postsecular, but its symbolic (and material) value was inseparable from the liberal principle of freedom of speech; the liberal fear of totalitarianism – commentators quoted Heinrich Heine's statement, 'Where they have burned books, they will end in burning human beings'; and the liberal conflation of religion and aesthetic value. The West, the 'free world' synonymous with civilization, bestows upon certain authors and artists an aura. They are fetishized. Dramatically pitched against this fetishism was the response by a worldwide Islamic community, many of whom had not read the book, but who nevertheless believed that

> The book contains distorted, unfounded, imaginary and despicable material about the Prophet of Islam, and the Islamic history. The Muslim concept of God, the character and personality of the Prophet of Islam, the lifestyle of the Companions of the Prophet of Islam, the sanctity of Muslim institutions of prayers and pilgrimage, and many other areas of Muslim religion, culture and history have been ridiculed with the sinister motive of portraying millions of Muslims all over the world as barbarians.[16]

And so the burning of Rushdie's book on that January afternoon in Yorkshire was viewed as announcing a cultural incommensurability in Britain itself.

In the media, the Muslim community (suddenly monolithic) appeared as those 'who did not understand the sacred role performed by literature in modern culture'.[17] There was a rush of statements outlining the character of British culture – John Patten's 'On Being British', most famously. The conservative politician Norman Tebbit asked which side would these Muslims support at cricket. The perceived threat triggered a discursive, literary counter-move that consisted in homogenizing British cultural history, repressing the diversity and alterities within the country (highly voluble under Major's government). If we return for a moment to Daniel Defoe we can see something of what is at issue here, not only in terms of postcolonial analyses, but also in terms of a pathology at the heart of cultural transformation after liberalism. For in January 1701 Defoe wrote a long poem entitled 'The True-Born Englishman', a satire responding to a poem by John Tutchin, 'The Foreignor'. In the poem he ridiculed English xenophobia and the absurdity of claiming a pure breed of Englishman. He emphasized how, following several conquests and waves of immigration, the British were a mongrel race. In fact, given the history of subsequent migrations and interracial marriages, there is probably not a country in the world that can lay claim to a pure and uniform racial identity. And yet such definitions of the British character were formulated throughout 1989. It is as if the perceived threat itself by this transnational religion practised by legal citizens with substantial genetic relations abroad was to some monolithic unity of being British that had been cultivated from the nineteenth century empire-building onwards. In other words, the reaction to the book burning manifested a cultural pathology: the fetish of British identity was being stripped of its aura. The mask was slipping. The reaction demonstrated how much had been invested in a fantasy that was suddenly threatened with exposure. The reaction testified to a sudden glimpse of the mechanics of fetishism itself. Hence the conservative backlash – the way the publicity-hyped book burning was used as a means of pulling immigrants into line in political arenas such as education and local government. A rhetoric of 'violence' was produced in the wake of a perceived attack on the liberal value of high culture. Multiculturalism was subsequently conceived as breaking up historical values and hegemonic interests. But it was, significantly, a multiculturalism defined in terms of practices of devotion and belief that forced the recognition of differences, and fostered a politics and pathology for those differences. The otherness of the other was a religious otherness that previously had gone unnoticed by most people.

The analysis offered here does not wish simply to turn the tables: castigate the British and exonerate the Muslims. On the one hand, that would be an 'Orientalist' move. Edward Said has himself been criticized by postcolonial theorists such as Homi Bhabha for constructing Islam as a victim of Western projection. Such victimage is paralysing. On the other hand, it is the very fact that these Muslims were themselves British citizens that renders the attribution of blame and guilt more complex. The Muslims of Bradford were caught up

143

in a violence that was in part engendered by the unreflective nature of Western liberalism – in fact, the very nature of Western liberalism. But that does not mean that their own position was a reflected one, only that it was a reactive one; that is, working in accordance with the same logic. The events of 14 January 1989 no doubt caused as much rethinking among British Muslims as it did among other British people who were not Muslims. The point is that the politics of difference generates guilts and blames on all sides. It points up liberalism's hidden imperialism as it operated in the past and, despite its appeal to egalitarianism, how it remains in force today. It also points up the compromised positions of those caught between two incommensurate cultures each demanding full allegiance. For both the British Muslims and the British non–Muslims the politics of difference, while calling into question the representations and images of the other, can make it impossible to discuss the 'other' at all (even, especially, when they are manifestly part of the same national society). The politics of difference produce, then, both apartheids and paralysis. It can reinforce a ghettoization, rendering us all victims of the way we represent ourselves to each other. We can become products of our own generated mythologies, caught up with the fetishisms of faith, while being critical of the ways others represent us. Caught in a cycle of exaggerating the differences to substantiate our distinctiveness while defending these self-representations against 'outsiders', can make us blind to the extent of our interdependencies. Levels of xenophobia and paranoia rise, fed and crystallized by the terrorist acts of freedom fighters.

The present cultural conflict within which religion figures is not the clash of civilizations Huntington foresees.[18] It is an internal conflict involving complex, hybrid sets of circumstance. It concerns the recognition of the immanent and irresolvable webs of guilt, violence and arbitrariness out of which we must necessarily construct our sense of the world. Yearning for transcendence, in a world riddled with the disseminations of God-talk and religion, the body itself – the bodies of individuals, the social bodies, the ecclesial bodies, the national bodies – is wracked and tormented by the politics of radicalized difference, by cultural incommensurabilities, by voices and fragments of memory. A number of theorists have described postmodernity as a culture of schizophrenia; a culture expressing a radically decentred and performative subjectivity; a culture of *bricolage*. This finds its expression in the figure of the possessed body; the body at war because of the stranger, the foreigner, or the alien within.

Possessions

The body is at the centre of Rupert Wainwright's film *Stigmata* (1999). It is a body afflicted with the five wounds of Christ. Significantly, like Gibreel Farishta and Saladin Chamcha, it is the body of an 'unbeliever'. Frankie is a young Philadelphia hairstylist, tattooist and body-piercer who we first see staggering home from a club with a man she then has sex with. The opening scenes of the American city set up contemporary secularism: its casual superficiality, its hedonism, its lights, speed, glamour, aural and visual overloading, seediness, its concern with image, experience and pleasure. The filming is similar to Luhrmann's: visceral cutting shots, violent zooming, abrupt angled shots, superimposition of images, indie music, strobic lighting. It contrasts with the actual opening scene of the film: a poor village in Brazil where the sick and disabled congregate. A priest-scientist from the Vatican, Father Andrew Kiernan, has been sent here to investigate the miracle of a statue of the Virgin Mary that weeps tears of blood. The filming is colourful and intimate (close-ups of faces), the pace slow and ritualized. What links the two scenarios is a set of rosary beads owned by the old priest of the village church, whose funeral is taking place when the investigator arrives. The rosary is stolen by a young village boy and sold on the market to Frankie's mother. The rosary shifts, then, from being a holy object used in the prayerful observance of a faith to a commodity, a fashion accessory. In fact, when Frankie opens the package sent from Brazil she describes it as a 'necklace'. It is the circle of exchange, then, that associates these two worlds, each ignorant of the other's understanding of things. But what is significant about this film is that the dualism of secular and sacred is not maintained. The rosary becomes the means of the violent coming to belief – both for Frankie and for Father Kiernan (who had lost his faith, but finds it again through the miracle of the stigmata). The possession possesses and processes a change.

145

A character in Michel Serres's book *Angels: A Modern Myth* asks:

Do you really think that machine and technologies would be able to construct groups and change history if they were passive objects? . . . These biros, writing desks, tables, books, diskettes, console, memories . . . produce the group that re-members, that expresses itself, and, sometimes, thinks . . . [W]e could call them technical quasi-subjects . . . To consider them purely as objects derives from the basic contempt that we still have for human labour.[19]

This reconception of the animation of objects, this possession of possessions, announces not only the re-enchantment of the real, but also a critique of materialism itself. Serres has Marx's analysis of the processes of reification and fetishization in mind, from the opening chapter of *Capital*: 'A commodity appears at first sight an extremely obvious trivial thing. But its analysis brings out that it is a very strange thing, abounding in metaphysical subtleties and theological niceties . . . The mysterious character of the commodity-form consists therefore simply in the fact that the commodity reflects the social characteristics of men's own labour.' What reifies and fetishizes is exactly that 'basic contempt that we still have for human labour' to which Serres draws attention.

In *Stigmata* possession is a critique of the scientific reduction and medical materialism of the body (portrayed throughout the film in Frankie's visits to the hospital and Andrew's instrumental reasoning). Whereas objects of Roman Catholic worship in Luhrmann's *Romeo & Juliet* are isolated by the camera and filmed as exaggerated kitsch fetishes, in *Stigmata* they are returned to the faith practices from which they have been separated. The rosary for a Catholic is part of an economy of prayer, of communication. It transgresses any supposed boundaries between nature and grace. It is, as Serres would have it, a 'technical quasi-subject': a sacred prosthesis, an extension of the one who prays. The process this rosary triggers is the coming to belief. It is a coming to belief that can only be violent and disruptive as it tears through the layers of secular assumption and surmise. In a bar, looking for the man she had slept with and speaking to her girlfriend, Frankie shouts: 'Hey, do you know what's scarier than not believing in God? Believing in it. I mean, really believing in Him is a fucking terrifying thought.' The terror of coming to belief is dramatically presented in receiving each of the five wounds of Christ: nails in the wrists and feet, the scourging of the back, the imposition of the crown of thorns, and the sword that pierces the side and heart. Frankie is forced to undergo an *imitatio Christi*. Father Alameida, who had owned the rosary, had himself experienced something if the stigmata. But although there are moments in the film when it seems Frankie is possessed by the spirit of Father Alameida, there is also the insistence that this priest is only a messenger: the source of the possession, and the only one besides St Francis to undergo all five wounds, is Christ himself. In the giving of each of the wounds, the portrayal is intercut with images of the crucifixion. In this way the young punk hairstylist from Philadelphia is inscribed within the traditions of the Catholic faith, in fact the traditions of Catholic sanctification (in the woundings there are montage shots of blood mingling with water and different characters allude to the smell of flowers). By the end of the film Frankie is walking, draped in white, in a misty garden in the early morning (echoes of the resurrection), a dove having rested upon her hand in the manner of St Francis/Frankie. There are statues of St Francis and St Clare in the garden.

We can appreciate the cultural distance 'religion' has travelled in this film by briefly comparing it to the most famous film about possession, William Friedkin's *The Exorcist* (1973). In fact, there are special-effect scenes in *Stigmata* that pay homage to this predecessor (and Polanski's *Rosemary's Baby*). *The Exorcist* also links the supernatural with the natural through an object, this time the small sculptured head of a demon, unearthed in Iraq. But nothing further is made of the object in the film. There is no exchange dramatized. Without explanation the head is next seen in the house of the unmarried movie actress, Chris MacNeil, and her pre-pubescent daughter, Regan, as an ornament – and then is never seen again. The lack of mediated exchange is emphasized by the jump-cut from Iraq to Chris's home (where 'rats' are heard in the attic). The technical jump-cut parallels the number of metaphysical dualisms that structure the narrative: the possession is by Satan–the exorcist, Merrin, the Catholic representative of the power of Christ;

evil–good; body–soul; darkness–light; bottom of the steps–Regan's attic room; the virginity of the child–the sexual explicitness of the demonic; cleanliness and organization–vomited filth and poltergeist chaos; male power and autonomy–female empathy and sociality. What is most prominent is how fear of penetration by the other – and hence the demonization of the other – preoccupies the film. This fear of penetration maintains a strict boundary between the internal body and the external body. When the possession transgresses that boundary, it is the exorcism that re-establishes it. The exorcism is a purgation, not of the fear but the source of the fear – a vicious and malevolent father-figure. The abusive father is displaced, projected onto the priest Father Karras who is thrown from Regan's bedroom window and plunges down the steps outside to his death. The women are left and peace is re-established in the home and in the body. The alien penetrator has been cast out, abjected beyond the walls.

The role the Catholic faith plays in *The Exorcist* is guardian and maintainer of domestic peace – a social peace achieved through the expunging of masculine presence, the other. The priests (Fathers Merrin and Karras) as celibates are castrated males – males who know of their penetrative powers and who have renounced them. They are not working priests – in parishes, in archdioceses, part of the papal and ecclesial institution. They are religiously marked functionaries, 'safe' men – like the male domestic help in Chris's bourgeois house who is told to see to the 'rats'. The social peace established by their emasculated ministrations is precarious (Regan is on the verge of womanhood) and sterile (Regan has no father, Chris no husband and the love interest is asexual). But Chris herself (a secularized Christ figure) is strong and independent. We first see her acting the part of a student demonstration leader in her latest film, 'Crash Course'. She is fighting on behalf of the right to education in the face of a threat to pull the buildings down (Georgetown Catholic University). In the fight for what she believes in – education for all, her daughter, her future – she will triumph. She will keep the enemy outside the gates. 'Military off Campus' reads one of the placards – as President Nixon was drafting home as many troops as possible from Vietnam. Liberal, democratic America will be maintained by exorcising radical difference from public space. This was

148

that lagoon-time between Nixon's Republican landslide, winning him a second term of office (1972), and the breaking of the Watergate scandal (1974). Liberal, democratic America will maintain its integrity (and unity) by castrating those who attempt to penetrate too far into its bourgeois soul. That includes the Catholic church: 'She remembers nothing', Chris tells Father Dyer as she and Regan are preparing to leave Georgetown. And a talismanic keepsake left by Father Karras is handed to Father Dyer as Chris and Regan drive away. The church is back in the closet. It is as if there had been no threat; packing the house and moving away is the final erasure of the past. What seals the domestic, feminized peace of liberal America is the strict maintenance of boundaries and a profound forgetting. What is most forgotten, hidden among the millions of frames, is the sculptured head of the demon that began it all: that is, the power of commodity fetishism itself.

The possession in *Stigmata* occurs because of the absence of boundaries; the bodies are permeable. The other, while seemingly evil (in that it terrorizes and is even treated as evil by the Vatican officials), is the spirit of God in Christ. The institution of the church – represented by Cardinal Houseman ('the cornerstone of the faithful is the church') – is seen maintaining the good–evil, male–female, clerical–lay, power–impotence divisions. However, finally, Father Andrew overcomes the powers of repression in the church that enforced such thinking. The one who is cast out in this film is Cardinal Houseman, who had concealed the discovery of a new gospel in Jesus's words, being translated by the saintly Father Alameida.

Furthermore, the fear of penetration is also overcome. From the beginning, with Frankie's coupling with the man she meets at the club, to the actual wounding itself, a pleasure is involved in being penetrated. The pleasure is sexual and beatific – as Frankie tells her girlfriend, 'I'm fucked'. The isolated body is brought into relation, even violently, with other bodies: objects, birds, the body of writings hidden by Father Alameida. In this relationality there is a transcendence and ecstasy. And despite the violence of the wounding, Frankie experiences no pain. The doctors comment on how normal her pulse and blood pressure remain. The permeability of the body is represented by the flight of doves and the dripping

149

of water into bowls and baths and pools and puddles. Messages are transmitted through the interpenetration of things corporeal. Reification, the commodity as fetish – that takes forms as diverse as the sacred relic of the 'new' gospel, the autonomy of the secularized individual and the defensive stronghold of the church as an institution (tyrannically maintained by Houseman) – is resisted. There is a rejection of the institution that takes itself too seriously and its power too literally, and a struggle against a certain doctrinal fundamentalism that arises from power-based interpretations of foundational documents. And yet this differs from modernity's anti-clericalism in that it does not espouse the secular as an alternative route to salvation; it does not reduce religion to a mystical and solipsistic experience of the Void; it does not accept postmodernity's adrenalin rushes and pop transcendence; it does not embrace New Age self-enlightenment therapies that conflate surrender with relaxation. Belief comes through pain and terror that act as technologies of selfhood (as Michel Foucault might say). In the course of the film Frankie becomes unable to drink alcohol, smoke or have sex. But – and this is significant for the way the theological is being seen today – these 'technologies' are now operating through the transmission of the tradition, not simply institutional governance. They issue from the transmission of traditionally held identifications between bodies. For example, the crucifix on the rosary is enacted in Frankie's life; the words of the 'new' gospel are announced through Frankie's lips and scrawled upon the walls of her flat; St Francis's act of relating to the birds is reperformed by Frankie in the garden; the votive candles in the church become the candles in the home; and the blood in the chalice becomes the blood being given as a transfusion in the hospital.

What is important in *Stigmata* for today's understanding of theology is the way the film stages the culture wars between liberal secularism and a certain theo-logic, but points to their resolution and perhaps also to the cultural destination towards which the West is moving. It is a move beyond postmodernity. For if we return to *The Exorcist*, the treatment of possession was concerned with an anal fixation in the West: the fear of penetration. And what is that fixation but the West's haunting by its own discovery, conquest and colonization programmes: the displaced imperialism of liberal universalism itself? What then is postmodernity but modernity enjoying its own pathological condition? Isn't this the implication of the move from Rothko to religion as special effect: the horror and the haunting become themselves sources of entertainment? And so the liquidation of religion turns itself into enjoying the absence of God. The tinted window of Chris MacNeil's Mercedes electronically seals her (and Regan) from the priest (who is walking) on the pavement. In her dark glasses and fur Chris is chauffeured away . . . to make another film.[20] *Stigmata* violently reverses that logic by affirming the terrifying presence and goodness of God – not as the remote figure of Enlightenment deism but as incarnate and visceral. It *is* quite specifically the Christian God, and the specificity is fundamental. The return to a theological tradition in opposition to the liquidation of religion must be a return to what Schleiermacher understood as the 'positive', material aspects of faithful practice. But the cultural trend of returning to faith communities I am tracing here need not be Christian. In a way, what Rushdie achieves in *Satanic Verses* has similarities with *Stigmata*. His is a much more sophisticated account of being possessed by a tradition. But that is what happens to Gibreel and Saladin. The Islamic faith throws both of them into cultural confusion and schizophrenia. Again coming to faith is a long traumatic affair, of voices, dreams, visions, hallucinations and the superimposition of one frame of reference upon another. Furthermore, the possession begins horrifically: the explosion by suicide-bombers of the flight from Bombay to London that was named after one of the gates in Paradise. As the two men tumble through the heavens in a litter of aircraft debris, at the opening of the novel, Gibreel shouts: 'To be born again . . . first you have to die'. There is worked out in both men a recognition that they are not secularized and autonomous individuals; they play a part in an unfolding theological drama. They are both actors after all. And as with Frankie and Father Andrew in *Stigmata*, the traditional faith that Gibreel ('I am the angel the god damned angel of god') and Saladin are returned to cannot remain the same. It is a tradition whose very health lies in the fact it can laugh at itself. That is, ironically, Rushdie's gift to Islam.

The opposite of possession in *The Exorcist* is the freedom of the liberal democrat. The opposite of possession in *Stigmata* and *Satanic*

151

Verses is dispossession; a dispossession breeding arbitrary violences, addictions to extreme stimulations and shallow entertainments. It would seem that, in a neo-tribal culture, only theological communities have the resources – in terms of history, tradition, transcendent truth-claims, and pedagogical practices for the formation of moral subjects – to resist the collapse into pragmatic and transitory values associated with media-driven 'lifestyles'. Only theological communities have the resources to cultivate forms of relationality that can resist the dissolving of the social into the cultural. There are other agencies – like the social and physical sciences – that can examine the extent of the webs of interrelation and dependence and stress the importance of understanding them. And these other agencies, which need not be based outside the theological communities, have a role in preventing the communities themselves fetishizing their faith and simply exacerbating neo-tribal association.

Nevertheless there is also an ambivalence about carrying through the radical theological reversal of secular logic in *Stigmata* – a hesitancy. And this is why I suggest we are still in a period of transition. It is as if the implications of the belief arrived at are still too frightening to face fully. For all the attention to the gendered body – close-ups of eyes and lips, mucous in the corner of the mouth, punctured limbs, bleeding, sensate and vulnerable flesh – Frankie's sanctity is through a mortification that stops as she wanders through the garden in the early morning. The statue of Francis is sentimental, naive; the colour of the filming is cold and formal. The 'new' gospel is identified, before the credits roll, with the Gospel of Thomas, a Gnostic text. It is this Gnosticism, involving the renunciation of the gendered body in favour of the soul, that reinstalls a dualism that the rest of the film has been struggling to overcome. The violence and terror of coming to belief seem to issue in a New Age dawn. To carry through the radical theological project would require Frankie returning to the city to live out her sanctity as a hairstylist, tattooist and body-piercer. The closing shots show Father Andrew, still very much the priest, back in the village church in Brazil locating the scroll Father Alameida had been translating so he can continue the work. Possibly this suggests the taking up of the 'other' into the tradition and rethinking (without abandoning) the tradition's orthodoxies in the light of it. That certainly is the only way beyond the liquidation of religion and the postsecular, postliberal cultural wars that follow in its wake; that too is the logical conclusion of *Stigmata*'s narrative: the uncompromising assertion of faith. But, in themselves, closely defined theological traditions could, once the common enemy of fundamental liberalism has been vanquished, lead to faith communities turning upon each other.

The Collocation of Faiths

The uncompromising assertion of Christianity will be matched by similar assertions from other faiths, other theological practices. And as long as each resists the fear of encountering the other and the different within itself, and the fear also of welcoming the stranger who is now the neighbour, then these communities will not cultivate but transfigure their resistance identities. Neither will they reify and fossilize the faith that is shared and dynamic among them. The very truth of each religion will be guaranteed by the other faiths that call it into question. The truth of the religion is a claim constituted in its very impossibility; a claim both made and humbled. This will announce a certain fideism – but not modernity's fideism that played itself off against scientific rationalism and a disenchanted world. This will be a fideism of the faithful, the committed ones, in a world of possibilities. The Imam already lives next door to the Orthodox priest, the Quaker shares a taxi with the Christian evangelical, the Rabbi sits on a civic board beside the Sikh. Words slip and slide. We have watched them: good/goods; consummation/consumerism; possession/possessed. Time passes. And, who knows – I said I thought we were in a place of transition – maybe as each active tradition recognizes their interdependence, and the sacred spaces that each shares and lives (though differently understood), then there will be fruitful interrelations between communities, shared projects for mutual flourishing, the slipping and sliding of interests. The true religion that each faith community practices and disseminates will then be inscribed within the world and redeem the spiritual materialisms of virtual reality or the omnivorous rule of global capitalism. As the prophet wrote: 'Without a vision the people perish'.

Afterword

The shadows of the twin towers of the World Trade Center stretch across this whole work, yet I have remained silent about the events in the United States on 11 September 2001. That demands an explanation, on moral grounds. I am not certain I can ever provide such an explanation. This is by way of one. I was returning to the University of Manchester, after attending a conference on Paradise, when the news broke. The partner of a close friend attending the same conference was among those missing. Later, at home, I sat dumbstruck by the reports, horrified by the pictures. I can still see those people waving from the floors above the black gashes left by the exploding aircraft. I still find myself thinking about what I would have done in their position. Throughout, I absorbed the news convinced that something did have to be said about 'religion' in the contemporary world. But what I could not do was weave 11 September into my narrative *as if* I understood the part it played in the unfolding logic of 'true religion'. I am not at all sure that I do understand. I remember nothing of my movements in the streets of Manchester that day, or my ride on a bus, or my journey by train. I recall only my profound sense, as I went to bed that evening, that I wasn't sure what the world would look like in the morning. As it happened, it was blue and clear and fine. I hope I don't take that for granted. We walk on water – but walk we must. And even now 11 September 2001 is being woven into other narratives – for that day too, maybe that day above all, must not be reified.

For those who died that day, their families, friends and colleagues, and for the people of Afghanistan.

Notes

1 Religion Before and After Secularism

1 Stephen Greenblatt, with respect to analysing what he calls the 'circulation of social energy', in *Shakespearean Negotiations* (Oxford: Clarendon Press,1988), p. 5.

2 This approach to Shakespeare's writings had been advocated in the 1970s by Peter Milward, but more recently became more popular. Anthony Holden in his recent biography *William Shakespeare: His Life and Work* (London: Abacus, 1999) devotes attention to it, and more scholarly attention has been given by E. A. J. Honigman, Richard Wilson and Velma Bourgeois Richmond.

3 Wilfred Cantwell Smith, *The Meaning and End of Religion* (New York: Mentor Books, 1962), p. 33.

4 From this we can observe that the changing understanding of the word 'religion' from premodernity to modernity was not simply a matter of Protestantism erasing a traditional Catholic past.

5 John Carey, *John Donne: Life, Mind and Work* (London: Faber and Faber, 1981), p. 24.

6 Jean Baudrillard, *Simulacrum and Simulation*, trans. Sheila Faria Glaser (Ann Arbor: University of Michigan Press, 1994), pp. 80–1.

7 'The Vision Machine' in *The Virilio Reader*, ed. James Der Derian (Oxford: Blackwell, 1998), p. 135.

2   True Religion and Temporal Goods

1   Kirkpatrick Sale, *The Conquest of Paradise: Christopher Columbus and the Columbian Legacy* (London: Macmillan, 1990), p. 5.

2   David Norbrook, in *The Court Masque*, ed. Lindley (Manchester: Manchester University Press), p. 97.

3   Stephen Toulmin, *Cosmopolis: The Hidden Agenda of Modernity* (Chicago: University of Chicago Press, 1990) p. 53.

4   Stephen J. Lee, *The Thirty Years' War* (London: Routledge, 1991), p. 2.

5   See Pierre Manent, *The City of Man*, trans. Marc A. LePain (Princeton, NJ: Princeton University Press, 1998).

6   Maximillian E. Novak, *Daniel Defoe: Master of Fictions* (Oxford: Oxford University Press, 2001), p. 103.

7   Max Weber, *The Protestant Ethic and the Spirit of Capitalism*, trans. Talcott Parsons (London: Routledge, 2001), p. xxxiii.

8   Mary Poovey, *The History of the Modern Fact: Problems of Knowledge in the Sciences of Wealth and Society* (Chicago: University of Chicago Press, 1998), p. 196.

9   Diana Loxley, *The Problematic Shores: The Literature of Islands* (New York: St Martin's Press, 1990), p. 10.

10 See E. Dahl, *Die Kurzungen des 'Robinson Crusoe' in England Zwischen 1719 und 1819* (Frankfurt: Peter Lang, 1977).

3   True Religion and Consumption

1   *Pensées* was not published until 1670. It is interesting to note the cultural connections between the dark infinities of Pascal's Catholic Jansenism and the Romantic understanding of God. Melville's writing, in *Moby Dick*, weds the Jansenist and Calvinist worldviews with a gothic Prometheanism.

2   The word 'kenosis' is Greek and is the noun form of the verb *kenoō*: to empty. Theologically it refers to the idea expressed in Paul's letter to the Philippians that Christ surrendered his kinship with the father out of obedience. He emptied himself of divinity to be made incarnate, died on the cross and rose again to sit once more at the side of the father in glory.

3   Novalis actually narrates the dramatic relationship between Eros, Fable, and Ginnistan (Imagination) in his allegorical novel *Heinrich von Ofterdingen*.

4 See Jacob Katz, *Out of the Ghetto: The Social Background of Jewish Emancipation, 1770–1870* (Cambridge, MA: Harvard University Press, 1973), p. 69.

5 Ibid., p. 54.

6 Andrew Bowie, *Aesthetics and Subjectivity: From Kant to Nietzsche* (Manchester: Manchester University Press, 1990), p. 24.

7 William James, *Varieties of Religious Experience: The Gifford Lectures 1901–2* (Glasgow: Collins, 1977) p. 414.

8 See Michel de Certeau, *The Mystical Fable*, trans. Michael B. Smith (Chicago: Chicago University Press, 1992).

9 Ibid., p. 49.

10 Talal Asad, *Genealogies of Religion: Discipline and Reasons of Power in Christianity and Islam* (Baltimore, MD: Johns Hopkins University Press, 1993), p. 48.

11 It would be worth comparing Schleiermacher with Hegel at this point, both of whom reject natural religion in any of its guises.

12 Introduction to *On Religion: Speeches to its Cultured Despisers*, ed. and trans. Richard Crouter (Cambridge: Cambridge University Press, 1988), p. 70.

13 See my *Cities of God* (London: Routledge, 2000), pp. 137–46 for an account of some of the rethinking that has been done recently and how Hegel is increasingly coming to be seen less as a philosopher and more as a major theologian.

14 Although it must be noted that Schleiermacher and Hegel share much in common and exaggerated the differences between them. Both begin with the relation of the finite to the infinite, for example, and both are concerned with forms of 'God consciousness' and the way that determines and transforms communities through Christ. Both also see Christianity as the religion in which religion itself reflects upon its own nature – and it is on this ground that, as a religion, Christianity's superiority rests.

15 Like Schleiermacher, Hegel was a liberal rather than a republican. Following the Prussian edict of 1812 emancipating the Jews there had been several attempts to draw back from the full implementation of the bill and to require Jewish people to convert to Christianity if they were to hold any state office (a professorship, for example). Neither Schleiermacher nor Hegel supported such a policy. In fact, throughout the time of the writing of Hegel's *Lectures on the Philosophy of Religion*, Hegel developed intimate friendships among the Jewish Berliners, including the jurist Eduard Gans and the satirist Moishe Saphir. In a letter to his wife he referred to Gans as 'my true friend

and companion'. While advocating the superiority of the Christian faith, then, neither supported state coercion.

16 See Rudolph Otto, *The Idea of the Holy: An Inquiry into the Non-Rational Factor in the Idea of the Divine and Its Relation to the Rational* (Oxford: Oxford University Press, 1950).

17 See Nathaniel Philbrick, *In the Heart of the Sea* (London: HarperCollins, 2000).

18 C. L. R. James, *Mariners, Renegades and Castaways: The Story of Hermann Melville and the World we Live In* (London: Allison and Busby, 1953).

19 Francis Fukuyama, *The End of History and the Last Man* (London: Hamish Hamilton, 1992).

20 This is the view of religion as it is investigated by twentieth-century anthropologists. For Mary Douglas, a 'person without religion would be the person content to do without explanations': see her *Implicit Meanings* (London: Routledge and Kegan Paul, 1975), p. 76. For Clifford Geertz, religion – conceived in terms of religious symbolism – negotiates 'at least three points where chaos – a tumult of events that lack not just interpretations but *interpretability* – threatens to break in upon man'. Geertz, *The Interpretation of Cultures* (New York: Basic Books, 1973), p. 100.

4   True Religion and Special Effect

1 D. Stephen Long, *Divine Economy: Theology and the Market* (London: Routledge, 2000), p. 55.

2 See Mark C. Taylor, *About Religion: Economies of Faith in Virtual Culture* (Chicago: University of Chicago Press, 1999), pp. 140–67.

3 Jean Baudrillard, *The Transparency of Evil: Essays on Extreme Phenomena*, trans. James Benedict (London: Verso, 1993), p. 3. Since liberation is at the heart of the liberal project then Baudrillard's statement is a description of the postliberal condition. That does not mean that all the liberal dreams are fulfilled, or about to be fulfilled – though there are some thinkers like Fukuyama who think we're close. Baudrillard is pointing to a post-PC culture where the language of liberation – for lesbians, gays, women, the poor, animals, ethnic and religious minorities, trees – is mouthed by those who seem to be quoting lines from a rather dated play. With rights for everything and everyone, then the language of rights implodes. Liberalism's Dionysian ecstasies are over – we have little white pills instead.

4 James E. B. Breslin, *Mark Rothko: A Biography* (Chicago: University of Chicago Press, 1993), p. 464.

5 Barbara Novak and Brian O'Doherty, 'Rothko's Dark Paintings: Tragedy and Void' in *Rothko* (New Haven, CT: Yale University Press, 1998), pp. 264–81 (273).

6 Breslin, *Mark Rothko*, p. 484.

7 There is one important difference between the Rothko Chapel and its aesthetic environment and a theme park: entrance to the chapel is free. Of course it is paid for in other ways – filtered through the complex capillary tubing of the tax-benefit system – and all donations are themselves 'tax deductible'. There is no free lunch. But the costing is invisible and 'the town of art' offers itself generously to the public.

8 Mark C. Taylor gives an account of another scheduled project, a 'Holy Land' constructed in the Nevada Desert. Plans were going ahead as he wrote, but I can find no further details.

9 Slavoj Žižek, *On Belief* (London: Routledge, 2001), pp. 12–15.

10 Owen Chadwick, *The Secularization of the European Mind in the Nineteenth Century* (Cambridge: Cambridge University Press, 1975), p. 21.

11 For a more detailed account of this process see my 'Introduction: Where we Stand' in Graham Ward (ed.) *The Blackwell Companion to Postmodern Theology* (Oxford: Blackwell, 2001).

12 The essay, translated by Samuel Weber, is available in Jacques Derrida and Gianni Vattimo (eds) *Religion* (Cambridge: Polity Press, 1998), pp. 1–78. The collection is significant for the argument presented here, for its origins lay in a conference on the island of Capri discussing the contemporary 'religious revival'.

13 Mark Edmundson, *Nightmare on Main Street: Angels, Sadomasochism and the Culture of the Gothic* (Cambridge, MA: Harvard University Press, 1997), pp. 67–8.

14 Roland Robertson, 'Globalization Theory and Civilizational Analysis', *Comparative Civilizations Review* 17 (Fall 1987), 22.

15 I take this term from James Davison Hunter, *Culture Wars: The Struggle to Define America* (New York: Basic Books, 1991). Hunter's concern is with 'the competing moral visions' between the religious 'orthodox' and the religious 'progressives' in public life in 1990s America. Here conviction is at war with conviction on issues such as abortion, gay rights and education. I have learnt much from his thesis, but my argument would suggest we are further along the line. Over ten years later that 'progressive' conviction, I suggest, is on the decline, exhausted by what has been termed 'compassion fatigue'.

Progressives have been fighting on too many fronts. What progressives remain have an entertainment value in debates with the orthodox (which is a much stronger lobby). They are nostalgic reminders and simulations of a 1970s identity politics.

16 A letter from a local Muslim sent to the *Telegraph and Argus*.

17 Talal Asad, *Genealogies of Religion: Discipline and Reasons of Power in Christianity and Islam* (Baltimore, MD: Johns Hopkins University Press, 1993), p. 302.

18 Samuel P. Huntington, *The Clash of Civilizations and the Remaking of World Order* (New York: Simon and Schuster, 1996), p. 70. Huntington's thesis is that global politics after the Cold War (in the 1990s and the new millennium) focuses on civilizations – the Western, the Islamic and the Chinese, in particular. The universalism of the West (recentred on the USA), the militancy of the Muslim world and the aggression of the Chinese will generate irresolvable conflicts, clashes between civilizations. We are threatened with a 'global Dark Ages' unless commonalities are sought and affirmed. In fact, it would seem that coexistence is only possible through dialogue, learning from each other and studying each other's history and ideals. While sympathetic to some of Huntington's analyses, my own examinations suggest the boundaries between civilizations cannot be defined so neatly. Waves of immigration (which he acknowledges) and the global mobilization of labour resist the homogenization particularly of Western universalism and Islamic militancy. Future coexistence, on my account, would issue from a more radical syncretism that would enable each of us to understand the extent of our interdependence.

19 Michel Serres, *Angels: A Modern Myth*, trans. Francis Cowper (Paris: Flammarion, 1993), p. 48.

20 There is another ending (the original) to the film, but this was cut. It has Father Dyer and the police lieutenant walking away in a new found friendship of church and state.

Index